Quick and Easy
Weaning

All you need to know on feeding your baby in the first year

10 9 8 7 6 5 4 3 2 1

Published in 2014 by Ebury Press, an imprint of Ebury Publishing
A Random House Group Company

Text © Annabel Karmel 2014
Photography © Dave King 2014
Illustrations © Gwénola Carrère 2014

Annabel Karmel has asserted her right to be identified as the author of this Work in accordance with the Copyright, Designs and Patents Act 1988

All rights reserved. No part of this publication may be reproduced, stored in a retrieval system, or transmitted in any form or by any means, electronic, mechanical, photocopying, recording or otherwise, without the prior permission of the copyright owner.

The Random House Group Limited Reg. No. 954009

A CIP catalogue record for this book is available from the British Library.

The Random House Group Limited supports The Forest Stewardship Council® (FSC®), the leading international forest-certification organisation. Our books carrying the FSC label are printed on FSC® -certified paper. FSC is the only forest-certification scheme supported by the leading environmental organisations, including Greenpeace. Our paper procurement policy can be found at www.randomhouse.co.uk/environment

Design by Smith & Gilmour
Photography by Dave King
Illustrations by Gwénola Carrère
Food and prop styling by Emma Lahaye

Printed and bound in China by C&C Offset Printing Co., Ltd

ISBN 9780091940287

Contents

First tastes: 6 months 4

After first tastes: 6 months 34

6 to 9 months 52

9 to 12 months 94

Index 172
Acknowledgements 175
About the author 175

First tastes

Why wean your baby?

The transition to solid food from a diet of milk, whether breast or formula, is a gentle process that is largely dictated by your baby's needs and ability to eat foods of a different texture. Introducing solids is about offering new tastes and textures and adding bulk to your baby's diet, but it also makes sense to use this time to get them into good, healthy food habits.

Weaning can seem quite overwhelming when you are bombarded with information on when to start, what to feed and how much, as well as advice on how to identify and cope with allergies or food intolerances. If there is a history of allergy in your family or your baby suffers from eczema it is advisable to try and breastfeed for the first 6 months. My aim in this book is to guide you through each step of feeding your baby so that the process is calm and doesn't cause you or your baby any anxiety. The delicious recipes here will take you through every stage of their development, offering ideas that will appeal to every taste and keep broadening their food horizons.

It is in early childhood that eating habits and tastes are formed for life; babies grow more rapidly in their first year than at any other age, and so between 6 and 12 months you have a fantastic opportunity to get your baby to eat a variety of different foods and encourage them to try new flavours and textures.

When to wean

Introducing food is a big milestone in a baby's life, and it is not a fixed set of steps; some babies are ready to wean earlier than others and love the experience of trying new foods, whilst other babies take a while to adjust to this new way of eating.

Current government guidelines suggest that babies be introduced to solids from the age of 6 months. You might prefer to start before this if you think your baby is ready earlier, but do bear in mind that it is important not to give food before 17 weeks, as a baby's digestive system has not yet fully matured at that age. From 17 weeks onwards, many babies can tolerate first tastes, so if your baby is ready you can begin to gradually introduce solids.

It is important that your baby has begun to be introduced to solid foods by the age of 24 weeks, even if your baby was born prematurely. It is particularly important that babies born early wean no later than 6 months to help them get the extra nutrition they need to gain weight, and also because they have missed out on vital nutrients like iron that start to be stored in your baby's body in the last months of pregnancy.

The reasons for not delaying weaning until after 6 months are:

* A baby's iron reserves start to deplete at around 6 months, and breast milk and formula no longer provide iron and vitamin D at the levels your baby needs to develop healthily. Iron is an important factor in brain development, and can be found in food sources such as red meat, pulses and green leafy vegetables.

* Eating solid foods helps your baby's mouth and tongue develop and prepare for speaking.

* Up to the age of 6 months, babies readily accept new tastes. If you leave it too late, some babies can become resistant to accepting new foods.

* Your baby's kidneys can now cope with solid food, and has the digestive enzymes required to break it down and extract the nutrients needed.

Breast and formula milk are still very important at this stage, though; they are a 'complete' food for the first six months, providing them with the nutrients they need as well as liquid to keep them hydrated. Your baby's usual milk should continue to be given until they are 12 months old, but always after solids so that it does not fill them up before they eat.

How do I know if my baby is ready to wean?

Your baby will let you know when they are ready to move on from milk, you just need to be able to spot the signs! Good indicators are that they may be hungrier than usual and no longer satisfied by their usual breast or bottle feed, or possibly wake in the night when they previously slept through. Often they will start to show more interest in what you are eating and may even pretend to chew as they watch you eat. Having said that, babies often go through a growth spurt between 3 and 4 months and so sometimes they wake more at night because they are hungry and demand more frequent feeds. Don't take only this as your cue that they are ready for solids, look for a few more signs first. Babies should be holding their heads up and have fairly good control of their movements before they can eat solids.

Getting ready to wean

The first time you feed your baby solids can be a nerve-wracking experience. So find a relaxing, quiet place with no distractions and take it slowly, following your baby's pace. Every baby is different; some jump at the opportunity of trying new tastes and textures, while others may be more reluctant, but both of you will soon get the hang of it and enjoy trying new flavours.

Offering first foods

First foods should be simple: a single fruit, vegetable or cereal is best. Choose foods that are unlikely to cause an allergic response (see page 11), and fruit that is ripe and full of flavour.

Consistency: First purées should be semi-liquid, almost like a yogurt consistency, and smooth, with no surprise lumps, as this can be offputting for babies.

Vegetables: Sweet root vegetables make ideal first foods – they are naturally sweet and will purée to a lovely smooth consistency. Try sweet potatoes, carrots, parsnips, butternut squash, pumpkin or swede. These bright orange vegetables are packed with betacarotene, which is essential for your baby's growth, and to encourage healthy skin, good vision and strong bones.

Fruits: Try ripe apple, pear, banana, avocado, papaya, peach, melon and mango.

Cereals and grains: Begin with gluten-free cereals such as baby rice, millet and quinoa (in case your baby has a gluten intolerance).

BEST FIRST FOODS
- Carrot
- Sweet potato
- Butternut squash or pumpkin
- Swede
- Parsnip
- Apple
- Pear
- Banana
- Papaya
- Peach
- Mango
- Avocado
- Baby rice
- Millet

Raw or cooked?

Raw fruit and vegetables contain a great quantity of nutrients, but more than half of these can be lost in the cooking process, depending on how you cook them. That said, some vegetables, such as carrots and tomatoes, are actually better for us when cooked because we absorb more nutrients from them in that state. However, although raw foods are more nutritious, they are also higher in fibre, which can cause problems for little tummies as they can't properly digest it and may become bloated. So the best combination is to introduce a few soft, raw fresh foods (such as avocado and banana), but also lots of cooked vegetables until their weaning is established. (See the recipes on pages 16–33 for the best first fruits and veg for your baby.)

No-cook purées
Simple purées made from fruits such as banana, avocado and papaya are fantastic first foods because not only do they simply require mashing, and so are very simple to prepare, but they're also ideal for taking out and about as they do not need preparing and packaging up before you go.

Taking that first taste
To give yourself and your baby the best introduction to solids, pick the time when they will be most receptive. A good moment is usually about an hour after your baby's normal morning milk feed and after they have had a nap. You can sit your baby on your lap, in a bouncy chair or you may already have a high chair with a cosy insert to make sure that your baby is secure.

Make sure that the food is quite runny to begin with and not too hot, then offer them the spoon with just a little purée on it; if they don't like the spoon in their mouth you can dip a finger into the food and let them suck your finger instead.

To begin with don't worry about how much food your baby takes – the important thing is that they are regularly introduced to a variety of fresh nutritious new foods. Smile and make your baby feel at ease, but if they are really resistant to trying the food, take it away and try again another time – it should not become a battle.

Getting into a routine
Initially you need only to offer your baby solids at one meal a day, so choose which one works best for you – if you have older, school-age children, lunchtime might be the best time of day, when there are fewer distractions and less rushing around. As your baby adapts to the new way of eating, add another solid 'meal', perhaps within a week or two.

At first your baby may only eat one or two tablespoons of purée, but you can increase or reduce the amount you offer if they seem to want more or less. Be guided by your baby's response to feeding.

Milk
Breast or formula milk provides all the nutrients your baby needs for the first 6 months. Cow's milk isn't suitable as a main drink for babies under one year of age as it is low in essential vitamins such as iron. As the solid food intake increases, milk becomes a less major part of the diet, however, your baby should still be drinking about 500ml of milk a day as it is an important source of protein and calcium. Cow's milk can be used in cooking or with cereal after 6 months instead of your baby's usual milk.

Between 4–6 months babies should have 500–600ml/18fl oz breast milk or infant formula milk each day, and this is still enough when your baby is first introduced to solids. Up to the age of 8 months, your baby needs to drink at least four times a day. Don't use softened water or repeatedly boiled water when making your baby's bottle, because of the danger of concentrated mineral salts.

Water

Babies lose more water through their skin and kidneys than adults, therefore it is vital that they take in enough fluids and don't become dehydrated. Ensure your baby drinks well throughout the day; cool, boiled water is the best drink to give on hot days. Avoid bottled mineral water as it contains high concentrations of mineral salts, which are unsuitable for babies. It isn't necessary to give young babies anything to drink other than milk or plain water if they are thirsty. If your baby refuses to drink water you can give unsweetened baby juice or fresh 100-percent fruit juice diluted to one-part juice to three-parts water.

Foods to avoid

In the first year your baby's food should not include any artificial colourings, flavourings, salt or sugar, but there are also some ingredients that should be avoided while your baby is still young.

Eggs: Babies can eat eggs from 6 months, but they must be thoroughly cooked through – until both yolk and white are solid.

Honey: Honey should not be given to children under 12 months, as it can cause infant botulism.

Nuts: About one in fifty children in the UK are allergic to nuts. Peanuts and peanut products in particular can induce a severe allergic reaction (anaphylaxis) which can be life threatening. If there is a history of allergy in the family including hay fever, eczema or asthma, seek medical advice before introducing any type of nuts to your baby. For babies where there are no allergy concerns, peanut butter and finely ground nuts can be introduced from 6 months. However, whole and chopped nuts are not suitable before the age of 5 due to the risk of choking.

Unpasteurised dairy products: Milk, cheese and yogurt must be pasteurised to prevent the risk of bacterial infection. Avoid runny cheese such as Brie, or those with 'mould' such as blue cheese. You should also opt for full-fat dairy products rather than low-fat alternatives, as babies need proportionately more fat than adults due to their rapid growth rate.

Salt can cause long-term damage to your baby's body, in particular to her kidneys.

Processed meats are particularly high in salt so avoid giving these to your baby. Remember that babies aren't accustomed to salt and simply won't miss the taste as adults might. A tiny bit of salt is acceptable in cooking, but if you use stock cubes make sure they are very well diluted and look out for low-salt brands.

Allergies

Allergies occur when your baby's immune system becomes confused. Instead of ignoring harmless food proteins they trigger a reaction that causes a chemical called histamine to be released. This is responsible for the symptoms associated with skin rashes and swellings. The incidence of food allergies in babies is only about 6 per cent, however if you have a family history of allergy, such as a food allergy, hay fever, asthma or eczema, your baby is at increased risk. Babies who suffer from eczema often also have a food allergy.

There are several foods that account for most allergies. For normal healthy babies there is no evidence to suggest that weaning later than 6 months, or delaying the introduction of potentially allergic foods will affect the likelihood of developing allergies. Current advice is to introduce solids between 4 and 6 months, with no delay for allergenic foods. Do not remove key foods such as milk and wheat from your child's diet before consulting a doctor. If there is a history of food allergy in the family or if your baby suffers from eczema, you will need to be more cautious when introducing new foods, but there is no need to worry unduly about food allergies unless you have a family history.

Potentially high-risk foods:
* Milk and dairy products (yogurt, cheese, butter)
* Eggs
* Peanuts
* Tree nuts (e.g. almonds, Brazil nuts, walnuts, hazelnuts, cashews)
* Fish
* Shellfish
* Soy
* Wheat /gluten (found in flour-based products)
* Kiwis
* Sesame seeds

Children normally outgrow allergies to milk and egg, but some allergies may linger. Allergies to nuts, shellfish and fish are less commonly outgrown. Never be afraid to take your baby to the doctor if you are worried that something is wrong. Young babies' immune systems aren't fully matured and they can become ill very quickly. Food allergies can show in two ways in babies: immediate allergies result in itchy spots, swelling and, in rare severe cases, difficulty in breathing. Delayed allergies can result in the symptoms: eczema, reflux, colic or diarrhoea. Reactions can in some cases be more severe, causing anaphylaxis which can be life threatening. Some children have an adverse reaction to citrus or tomato. Allergy to tomato and citrus fruits is very rare, and the redness around the mouth this produces is the irritant effect of fruit acid.

SPOTTING THE SIGNS OF A SEVERE FOOD ALLERGY

✳ In rare cases a baby may experience a severe allergic reaction. If your baby goes pale, seems droopy or drowsy, experiences swelling in the face and neck and begins to have breathing difficulties, call an ambulance. Your baby could be suffering an anaphylactic reaction to something they have eaten and needs immediate medical assistance.

Cooking for your baby

While there are a great many products available to buy, homemade foods are always the best option, as you know exactly what has gone into them. Whether you are a beginner or an experienced cook, preparing delicious and nutritious food for your baby needn't be hard work.

Getting ahead can save you a lot of stress on a busy day, so every now and then, have a cooking session and prepare more than you need.

Batch cooking involves cooking larger quantities that can be divided into portions in ice-cube trays and then frozen in batches. Get into the habit of cooking extra portions of vegetables when cooking for yourself, too, as these can be puréed or mashed then frozen (but be careful to add salt only to your food, not to your baby's food). You can even make up combinations by freezing two individual flavours, such as apple and carrot, then defrosting them and mixing them together.

Freezing and reheating: Freezing batches of baby food means you always have something fresh and nutritious on hand to feed your baby. Once you have cooked the fruit or vegetables, purée them and then cover and allow to cool before freezing. Fill small pots or ice-cube trays almost to the top and store, covered, in a freezer that will freeze at -18°C or below within 24 hours. To thaw, take the food out of the freezer several hours before a meal and then reheat until piping hot. Allow to cool down a little before serving.

It is important to cook food thoroughly before giving it to your baby. If you are using a microwave to cook or reheat food, stir it carefully and watch out for 'hot spots' (some parts of the food may be hotter than others, so stirring will distribute the heat evenly). Do not refreeze meals that have previously been frozen and defrosted; the exception to this is raw frozen food such as frozen peas, which can be cooked then re-frozen.

Equipment

A little planning makes weaning your baby much easier, but you only need a few key items of equipment to prepare first foods. If you don't already have some of these things, choose a few that you think will help make mealtimes a quicker more positive experience for you and your baby.

Essential equipment

An electric hand blender: This is great for puréeing small quantities of baby food as well as larger quantities (which you can then freeze in small portions), and essential if you do not have a food processor or much cupboard space. You can pick these up easily and fairly cheaply. I like the ones that come with a tall plastic beaker, as these are perfect for puréeing up fruit and veg and mean you are less likely to splash the walls with food in the process!

An ice-cube tray: Freeze small portions of purées in ice-cube trays and press out a cube or two and leave to defrost whenever they are needed. Buy a flexible tray that has a lid, which you can stick a label on to remind you what is in each tray. Put the date of freezing on it too, to help you keep track of what you have in the freezer.

A masher: A potato masher is ideal for mashing food into lumpier textures as your baby moves on beyond first tastes. Try to get a mini masher, as this will make it easier to prepare small amounts of food.

A bib: Babies are messy, and weaning will never be a clean experience! Plastic wipe-clean bibs are useful to protect clothes, but choose one that fits under your baby's chin and is not too tight. Younger babies may find soft, cotton ones more comfortable.

A suitable chair: Ideally, choose a chair that will wipe clean easily and will support your baby's head. If your baby isn't quite ready for a high chair, just use their car seat (covered with a tea towel!) or baby seat.

Feeding spoons: Choose a soft, plastic spoon that is small enough to fit easily in your baby's mouth and has a long handle, and no sharp edges that may hurt your baby's gums. Get them holding the spoon from early on and let them try self-feeding, even if very little goes into their mouths at first!

Small bowls: Small food containers you can hold in one hand are very useful and ideally should be freezerproof and microwave-safe too. Choose ones with lids so you can transport food easily, and make sure they are dishwasher safe to make clearing up easier!

A lidded cup: From 6 months milk and other drinks should be offered in a cup rather than a bottle. Avoid the non-spill cups as these require sucking, which won't help your baby learn how to drink properly, and make sure the handles are soft and easy for your baby to hold on to. When drinking, the liquid should flow freely, but not too quickly to prevent choking.

Useful equipment

A food processor: Ideal for producing larger quantities of purées for freezing.

A steamer: This bit of kit makes cooking fruit, vegetables, fish and poultry really easy and it is also one of the healthiest ways to prepare food – for you and your baby! Steaming helps preserve essential nutrients, particularly water-soluble vitamins that would otherwise get lost in the cooking liquid. If you have a microwave, you can also steam food in a special microwave steamer.

A mouli (small food grinder): This is really useful for preparing foods with tougher skins, such as peas or dried fruit, so that you can separate the less digestible parts. Potato is much better puréed in a mouli rather than a food processor, as the result is much less sticky.

A mess mat: If you are feeding above a carpet or want to make clearing up easier after a meal, invest in a mess mat. When your baby has finished eating you can simply scoop it up and wash it rather than spending ages clearing up on your hands and knees! Place it under your baby's chair, and try to get one that is non-slip, stain resistant and wipe clean.

First tastes meal planner

Week 1

Day	Breakfast	Mid-morning	Lunch	Tea	Bedtime
Day 1–2	Breast/ Bottle	Breast/ Bottle	First veg purée eg: carrot or sweet potato	Breast/ Bottle	Breast/ Bottle
Day 3	Breast/ Bottle	Breast/ Bottle	Apple purée	Breast/ Bottle	Breast/ Bottle
Day 4	Breast/ Bottle	Breast/ Bottle	Baked butternut squash	Breast/ Bottle	Breast/ Bottle
Day 5	Breast/ Bottle	Breast/ Bottle	Mashed banana	Breast/ Bottle	Breast/ Bottle
Day 6	Breast/ Bottle	Breast/ Bottle	Trio of root veg	Breast/ Bottle	Breast/ Bottle
Day 7	Breast/ Bottle	Breast/ Bottle	Apple & pear	Breast/ Bottle	Breast/ Bottle

Week 2

Day	Early morning	Breakfast	Lunch	Tea	Bedtime
Day 1	Apple purée	Breast/ Bottle	Carrot purée	Breast/ Bottle	Breast/ Bottle
Day 2	Banana	Breast/ Bottle	Baked butternut squash	Breast/ Bottle	Breast/ Bottle
Day 3	Apple & pear	Breast/ Bottle	Trio of root veg	Breast/ Bottle	Breast/ Bottle
Day 4	Avocado & banana	Breast/ Bottle	Baked sweet potato	Breast/ Bottle	Breast/ Bottle
Day 5	Baby cereal & apple	Breast/ Bottle	Trio of root veg	Breast/ Bottle	Breast/ Bottle
Day 6	Baby cereal & pear	Breast/ Bottle	Baked sweet potato & butternut squash	Breast/ Bottle	Breast/ Bottle
Day 7	Banana & blueberry	Breast/ Bottle	Carrot & apple	Breast/ Bottle	Breast/ Bottle

First fruit purées

Suitable for freezing
Suitable from 6 months
Makes 2 portions

Cream of pear purée

Ingredients

2 ripe pears, peeled, cored and cut into chunks
1 tbsp baby rice
1 tbsp of your baby's usual milk

Ripe pears are naturally sweet and a good source of vitamin C, so they are a healthy first fruit for your baby. I particularly like using Conference pears for their juicy, sweet flesh. Some fruit purées, like pear and peach, are quite runny, but adding a little baby rice mixed with some of your baby's usual milk will give them a creamier taste and thicker texture.

✶ Put the pear chunks into a small saucepan then cover with a lid and cook for 2–3 minutes until tender. Blend to a smooth purée. Mix together the baby rice and milk and stir into the pear purée.

Suitable for freezing
Suitable from 6 months
Makes 4 portions

Apple purée

Apples are ideal first fruits as they are unlikely to cause allergies and can be blended to a smooth consistency that babies love. It's a good idea to taste the fruit first yourself to make sure it's naturally sweet before you prepare it.

✸ Peel, halve, core and chop the apples and put them into a heavy-based saucepan with the water or apple juice. Cover and cook over a low heat for 7–8 minutes until really tender.

✸ Purée in a food processor or in a bowl using an electric hand blender.

✸ You could also steam the apples for 7–8 minutes until tender. If steaming, add some of the boiled water from the bottom of the steamer when you blend the fruit, to thin out the purée.

Ingredients

2 dessert apples, eg: Pink Lady, Royal Gala or Jazz apples
4–5 tbsp water or pure, unsweetened apple juice

Banana and blueberry

Blueberries are one of the most antioxidant-rich foods in the world. These berries are one of only a few natural foods that are blue, and it is the pigment in their blue colour which provides most of its antioxidant properties. Blueberries are also a good source of fibre.

Ingredients

1 small ripe banana, peeled and sliced
30g (1oz) sweet blueberries
1 tbsp pure, unsweetened apple juice

✱ Put the banana in the saucepan together with the blueberries and apple juice. Cover and cook over a low heat for about 3 minutes until the blueberries burst open. Mix together to combine and allow to cool before serving.

Suitable from 6 months
Makes 1 portion

Apple and pear purée

Apple and pear blend well together, but if you want to introduce a new flavour to these familiar tastes, add a small cinnamon stick while the fruits cook and remove it before blending. Choose naturally sweet eating apples like Pink Lady, Jazz or Royal Gala.

Ingredients

2 dessert apples, peeled, cored and chopped
2 ripe pears, peeled, cored and chopped
3 tbsp pure, unsweetened apple juice
2 tbsp water

✱ Put the fruit into a heavy-based saucepan with the apple juice and water (or you could leave out the apple juice and use 5 tablespoons of water if you prefer). Cover and cook over a medium heat until tender, about 7–8 minutes. Blend the fruit until smooth.

Suitable for freezing
Suitable from 6 months
Makes 4 portions

No-cook baby purées
Suitable from 6 months

Weaning your baby doesn't have to mean a lot of effort and time spent in the kitchen; there are many delicious and nutritious purées that don't need any cooking at all...

Suitable for freezing
Suitable from 6 months
Makes 1 portion

Papaya

Papayas are a good source of betacarotene and vitamin C, are good for your baby's digestion, and are also a natural laxative, so can help with constipation.

Ingredients

½ small papaya

✶ Cut the papaya in half, remove the seeds and scoop out the flesh into a bowl. Mash the flesh with a fork until smooth.

Banana

Bananas are bursting with nutrients and make an ideal food for your baby as they are easily transportable. If you like, you can mix banana with other fruits like blueberries, peaches or pears. Once your baby is able to hold things and has reasonably good hand-to-eye coordination you can give her pieces of banana to chew on. A good tip is to cut the fruit in half, then simply peel some of the skin away to expose no more than 2cm of it. Let your baby hold the part of the banana with the skin on, otherwise it is difficult to grip and gets very mushy and messy!

Ingredients

½ small ripe banana, peeled
A little of your baby's usual milk (optional)

✶ Simply mash the banana with a fork until smooth. If this is too thick for your baby you can add a little of your baby's usual milk.

Suitable from 6 months
Makes 1 portion

Banana and peach

When ripe sweet peaches are in season they make great baby food because they are easy to digest and unlikely to cause an allergic reaction. To peel a peach, first bring some water to the boil in a saucepan, cut a cross in the base of the fruit, then boil in the water for 1 minute. Remove it with a slotted spoon and plunge into ice-cold water. Once the fruit is cool, you should find that the skin peels away quite easily. Diced peach also makes good soft finger food.

Ingredients

1 small ripe banana, peeled and sliced
1 small ripe peach, skinned, stoned and cut into pieces

✶ Simply mash together the banana and peach flesh.

Suitable from 6 months
Makes 1 portion

Mango purée

Mangoes are rich in antioxidants that help boost your baby's immune system, and are also a good source of vitamin C, which helps the body absorb more iron from other foods.

Ingredients
1 ripe mango

✶ The best way to peel a mango is to place the fruit on a chopping board with the stone positioned vertically. Using a sharp knife, slice the thickest part of the mango on either side of the stone, cutting around it as close as possible.

✶ Make about 3 horizontal and vertical cuts in the mango flesh, taking care not to cut through the skin. Pull down the sides and push up from the bottom of the mango half to fan the cut flesh so that the cubes pop up and separate. You can then slice off the cubes using a small sharp knife.

✶ Purée the flesh using an electric hand blender.

Suitable for freezing
Suitable from 6 months
Makes 2-4 portions

Banana and mango

Mango is good mixed with banana, adding a smooth texture and a deliciously sweet taste.

Ingredients
1 small ripe banana, peeled and sliced
75g (3oz) sweet, ripe mango, peeled and chopped

✶ Simply mash together the banana and mango until it reaches a smooth texture for your baby.

Suitable from 6 months
Makes 1-2 portions

Banana, peach and strawberry

Ingredients
1 small ripe banana, peeled and sliced
1 small ripe peach, skinned, stoned and chopped
2 strawberries, hulled and quartered

✶ Put the fruit into a saucepan and cook for 2 minutes. Purée using an electric hand blender.

Suitable from 6 months
Makes 1-2 portions

Avocado

Suitable from 6 months
Makes 1 portion

Avocados are rich in brain-boosting omega-3s and they have a mild flavour and velvety texture that babies like. An extra bonus is that they are full of good fats and have a high nutrient content. The way you peel it makes a difference to its nutrient levels, as their greatest concentration is in the dark green flesh that lies just beneath the skin. The best method is to cut all around the avocado lengthwise, take hold of both halves and twist them in the opposite direction until they separate naturally. Remove the stone and then cut each half lengthwise to produce four long quartered sections. Using your thumb and index finger, grip the edges of the skin and peel it off each quarter.

Ingredients

½ small ripe avocado
A little of your baby's usual milk

✶ Prepare the avocado. Mash the flesh together with a little of your baby's usual milk.

Avocado and banana

Suitable from 6 months
Makes 1 portion

It may seem strange but the combination of mashed avocado and banana is popular with babies. Adding ripe banana to this simple nutrient-rich purée gives it added and delicious sweetness.

Ingredients

½ small ripe avocado
½ small ripe banana

✶ Prepare the avocado. Remove the stone and then cut each half lengthwise to produce four long quartered sections. Using your thumb and index finger, grip the edges of the skin and peel it off each quarter. Peel and slice the banana and mash together with the avocado flesh.

Suitable for freezing
Suitable from 6 months
Makes 4 portions

First vegetable purée

Ingredients

2 medium carrots, peeled and chopped or sliced
A little of your baby's usual milk (optional)

Carrots make a perfect first food, packed with nutrients and having a sweet taste and smooth texture. You could use this recipe for other root veg, such as 1 medium sweet potato, peeled and chopped, 2 parsnips, peeled and chopped, ½ small swede, peeled and chopped. All orange-coloured root vegetables are a good source of betacarotene, the yellow/orange pigment that the body converts into vitamin A. We need vitamin A for healthy skin, good vision and a strong immune system.

✶ Put the carrots in a steamer. Cover and cook for 15–20 minutes until the carrots are really tender.

✶ Purée the carrots until smooth in a food processor or using an electric hand blender, adding a little water from the bottom of the steamer or some of your baby's usual milk to get a smooth consistency. First purées should be quite runny so that they are easy for your baby to swallow.

Baked sweet potato

Sweet potato is a fantastic source of betacarotene and many other nutrients, and baking it intensifies its natural sweetness. Unlike ordinary potatoes, sweet potatoes can be puréed in a food processor and their starches won't break down and develop a sticky texture.

Ingredients
2 medium sweet potatoes
 (approx 500g/1lb 2oz in total)
A little of your baby's usual milk (optional)

✱ Pre-heat the oven to 200C / 400F/ Gas 6.

✱ Scrub the potatoes and prick them all over with a metal skewer or fork. Place on a baking sheet and bake for about 1 hour or until tender.

✱ Remove from the oven, allow to cool a little and then cut in half. Scoop out the flesh and purée in a food processor or using an electric hand blender. You can add a little of your baby's usual milk to thin out the consistency if you wish.

Suitable for freezing
Suitable from 6 months
Makes 5 portions

Baked butternut squash

A good way to prepare butternut squash is to cut it in half and bake it in the oven. One of the advantages of this method is that you don't need to peel and chop the squash.

Ingredients
1 medium butternut squash (approx 700g/1½lb), halved and deseeded
A little sunflower oil
A little of your baby's usual milk (optional)

✱ Pre-heat the oven to 200C / 400F / Gas 6. Brush the sliced sides of the butternut squash with the oil, then put them, sliced side up, in a shallow ovenproof dish. Pour in some water around them – it should be about 1cm/ ½in deep. Bake the squash in the oven for 45 minutes to 1 hour or until tender.

✱ Remove the dish from the oven and allow the squash to cool down a little. Scoop out the flesh and purée to the desired consistency. You can add a little of your baby's usual milk if you wish.

Suitable for freezing
Suitable from 6 months
Makes 6 portions

Suitable for freezing
Suitable from 6 months
Makes 4 portions

Baked sweet potato and butternut squash

Two favourite vegetables in one. Baking these in the oven caramelises the natural flavour of these vegetables and adds a sweetness that babies like.

Ingredients

A little sunflower oil
225g (8oz) butternut squash, peeled and cubed
225g (8oz) sweet potatoes, peeled and cubed
A little of your baby's usual milk (optional)

* Pre-heat the oven to 200C / 400F/ Gas 6. Lay a large piece of foil on a baking sheet, brush with a little sunflower oil and spread the cubes of squash and sweet potato onto the foil. Brush the cubes with a little sunflower oil. Cover with a second large piece of foil and scrunch the edges of the two pieces together to form a parcel. Bake in the oven for about 30 minutes or until the vegetables are tender.

* Transfer to a food processor, including any liquid in the parcel, and purée until smooth. You can thin the purée with a little of your baby's usual milk if you like.

Suitable for freezing
Suitable from 6 months
Makes 4 portions

Trio of root vegetables

You can use any combination of root vegetables to make this. Root vegetables make the perfect weaning food because of their naturally sweet taste and smooth texture when puréed.

Ingredients

1 large carrot, peeled and diced
1 medium sweet potato (about 250g/9oz), peeled and diced
1 small parsnip (about 60g/2½oz), peeled and diced
A little of your baby's usual milk (optional)

* Put the vegetables in a steamer. Cover and cook for 15–20 minutes or until the vegetables are soft.

* Purée until smooth in a food processor or use an electric hand blender. Add a little water from the steamer or some of your baby's usual milk to get the right consistency if the purée is a little thick.

After first tastes

Once you have introduced your baby to a variety of single-ingredient first vegetables and fruits and some simple combinations, you can move onto some new combinations and tastes, like green vegetables. The best way to introduce these new flavours is to combine them with fruits or vegetables that your baby is already familiar with, such as sweet potato, carrot or apple.

After first tastes meal planner

	Early morning	Breakfast	Lunch	Tea	Bedtime
Day 1	Breast/ Bottle	Breast/ Bottle Apple, peach & blueberry	Butternut squash, carrot & apricot Breast/ Bottle	Parsnip & apple Water or diluted juice	Breast/ Bottle
Day 2	Breast/ Bottle	Breast/ Bottle Apple, pear & raisin	Sweet potato, broccoli & peas Breast/ Bottle	Butternut squash, sweet potato & pear Water or diluted juice	Breast/ Bottle
Day 3	Breast/ Bottle	Breast/ Bottle Cereal, apple & strawberry	Butternut squash, parsnip, apple & prune Breast/ Bottle	Carrot, parsnip & apple Water or diluted juice	Breast/ Bottle
Day 4	Breast/ Bottle	Breast/ Bottle Cereal & mango	Butternut squash, carrot & apricot Breast/ Bottle	Swede, apple & spinach Water or diluted juice	Breast/ Bottle
Day 5	Breast/ Bottle	Breast/ Bottle Apple, pear & raisin	Sweet potato, broccoli & peas Breast/ Bottle	Butternut squash, parsnip, apple & prune Water or diluted juice	Breast/ Bottle
Day 6	Breast/ Bottle	Breast/ Bottle Banana & blueberry	Carrot, potato & sweetcorn Breast/ Bottle	Carrot & apple Water or diluted juice	Breast/ Bottle
Day 7	Breast/ Bottle	Breast/ Bottle Cereal & peach	Butternut squash, parsnip, apple & prune Breast/ Bottle	Carrot, sweet potato & broccoli Water or diluted juice	Breast/ Bottle

Apple, pear and raisin

A tasty combination; the raisins and prunes are good if your baby has constipation.

Ingredients

2 dessert apples, peeled, cored and chopped
1 large ripe pear, peeled, cored and chopped
2 tbsp raisins
2 tbsp pure, unsweetened apple juice
Pinch of ground cinnamon (optional)

✳ Put everything into a saucepan, cover and cook over a medium low heat for about 7 minutes. Blend to a purée.

*Suitable for freezing
Suitable from 6 months
Makes 3 portions*

Apple and strawberry

You can introduce berries to most babies at around 6 months. Sometimes babies develop a rash after eating strawberries, particularly if they suffer from eczema, but don't worry if they do, this may not be a true food allergy. Strawberries are an excellent source of vitamin C.

Ingredients

2 dessert apples, peeled, cored and chopped
2 tbsp pure, unsweetened apple juice
50g (2oz) strawberries, hulled and quartered

✳ Put the apples into a saucepan together with the apple juice and cover and cook for 5 minutes.

✳ Add the strawberries and cook for a further 2 minutes. Blend to a purée.

*Suitable for freezing
Suitable from 6 months
Makes 2 portions*

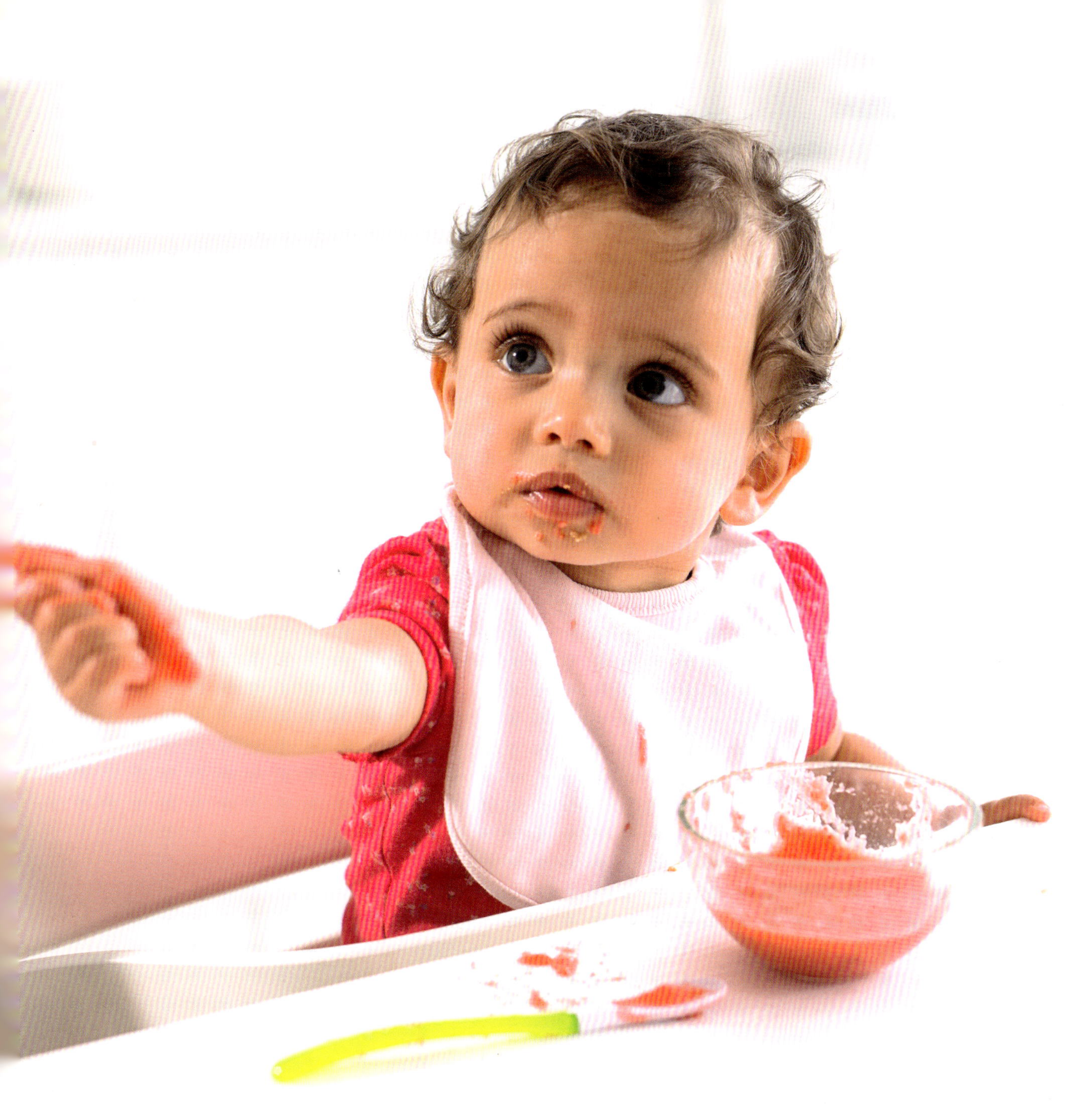

Suitable from 6 months
Makes 1 portion

Mango and peach

Another delicious no-cook combination. Make sure the mango and peach are ripe and sweet.

Ingredients

100g (4oz) fresh ripe mango, peeled and chopped (approx ½ a medium mango)
1 ripe peach, skinned, stoned and chopped
½ ripe banana (optional)

✸ Simply blend together the mango and peach. You can mix this purée with ½ small peeled and mashed banana, if you wish.

Suitable from 6 months
Makes 3 portions

Apple and mango

There are many different types of mango. They can be red, green or yellow. To tell if they are ripe, push gently on the skin; they should be slightly tender. If they are too hard, don't give them to your baby and if too soft they are over ripe. Best to taste yourself before giving to your baby.

Ingredients

2 dessert apples, peeled, cored and chopped
2 tbsp pure, unsweetened apple juice
100g (4oz) fresh ripe mango, peeled and chopped

✸ Put the apples into a saucepan together with the apple juice. Cover and cook for 7–8 minutes until tender. Purée with the fresh mango using an electric hand blender.

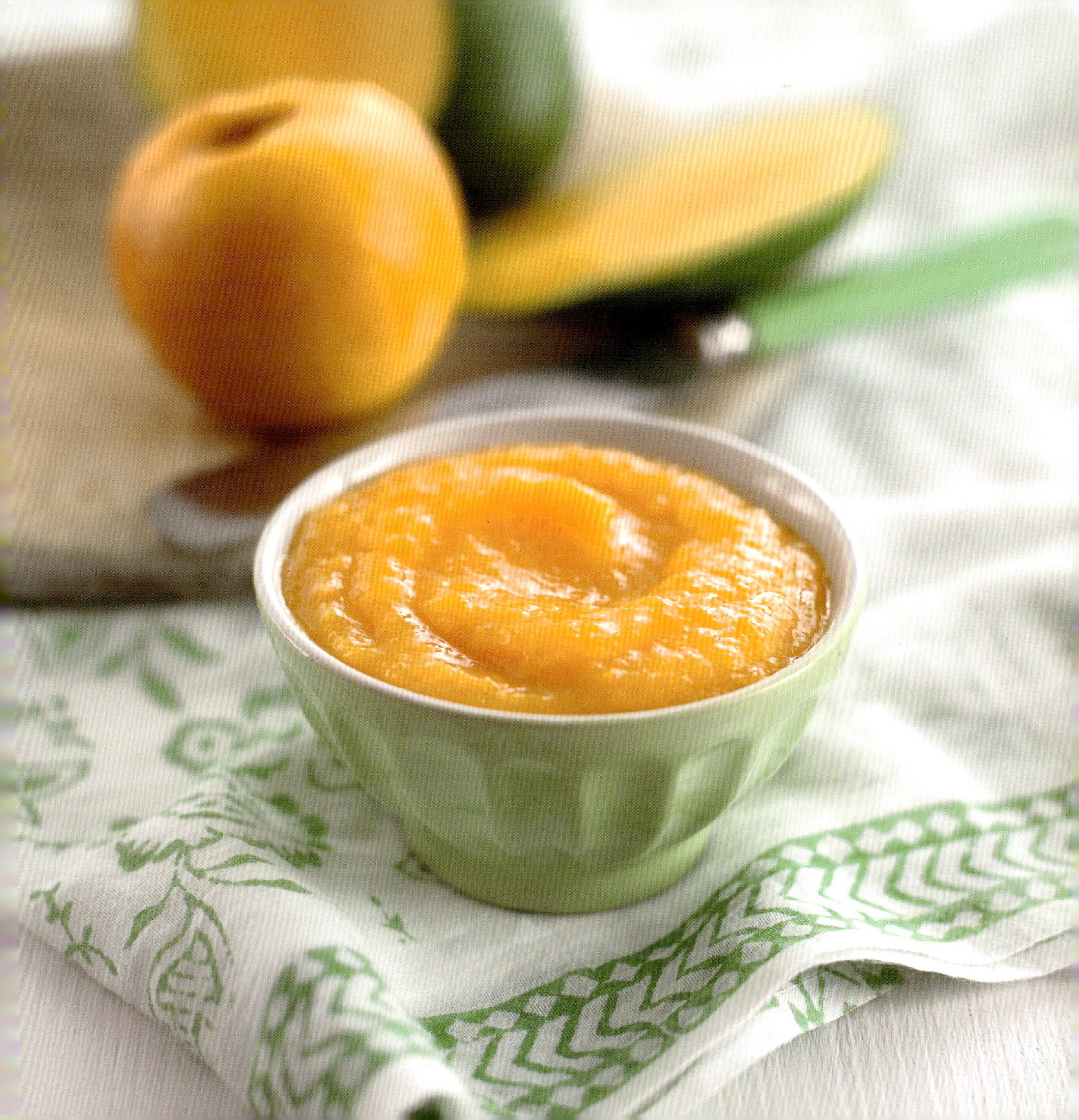

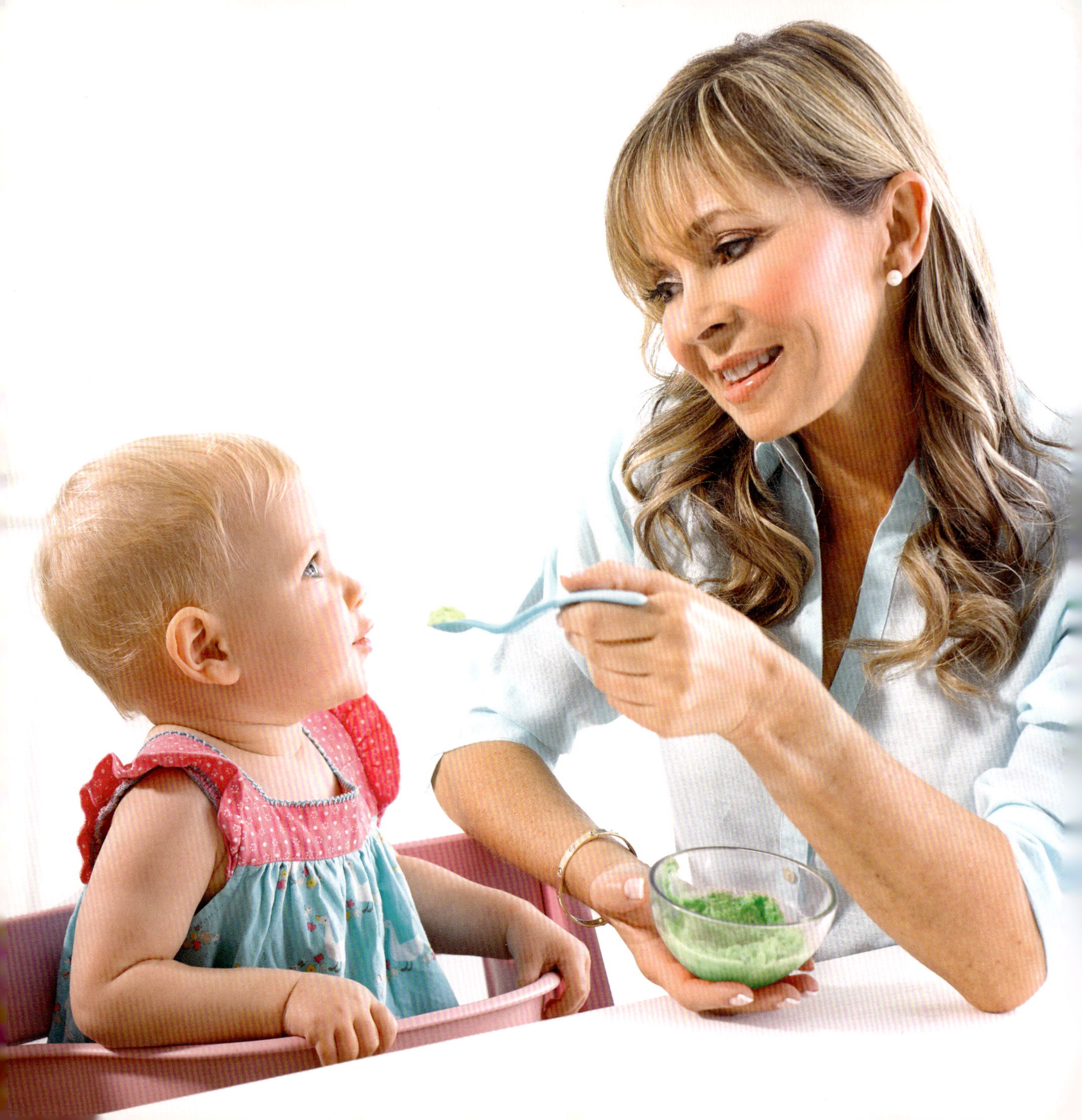

Swede, apple and spinach

Swede is often neglected as a food for babies, but it has a lovely earthy and creamy flavour. Mix it with sweet flavours such as carrot, butternut squash, apple or, as here, with some fresh spinach leaves.

Ingredients
300g (10oz) swede, peeled and chopped
1 dessert apple, peeled, cored and chopped
30g (1oz) baby spinach leaves, washed

✳ Put the swede and apple into a steamer, cover and cook for 8 minutes. Add the spinach and continue to cook for 2 minutes. Blend using an electric hand blender. You may need to add a little of the water from the steamer to make a smooth consistency.

Suitable for freezing
Suitable from 6 months
Makes 3 portions

Apple, peach and blueberry

Use sweet blueberries when making this purée. Peel the peach by cutting a cross in the base, plunge it into boiling water for a minute, then submerge in ice-cold water for 1 minute.

Ingredients
2 dessert apples, peeled, cored and chopped
2 tbsp pure, unsweetened apple juice
40g (1½oz) sweet blueberries
1 ripe peach, peeled, stoned and chopped

✳ Put the apples into a saucepan together with the apple juice. Cover and cook for about 6 minutes. Add the blueberries and cook for 3 minutes. Purée together with the peach using an electric hand blender.

Suitable from 6 months
Makes 2-3 portions

Butternut squash, carrot and apricot

You can save time when preparing this by buying ready peeled and chopped butternut squash.

Ingredients

200g (7oz) butternut squash, peeled and chopped
1 carrot, peeled and chopped (75g/3oz)
50g (2oz) soft, ready-to-eat dried apricots

✶ Put the squash, carrot and apricots into a steamer, cover and cook for 10–12 minutes or until they are all tender. Blitz to a purée together with 3 tablespoons of the water from the bottom of the steamer.

Suitable for freezing
Suitable from 6 months
Makes 2-3 portions

Butternut squash, sweet potato and pear

Combinations of vegetables and fruit tend to be popular with babies. You could also just use 250g (9oz) of butternut squash or sweet potato instead of a mix of squash and sweet potato.

Ingredients

150g (5oz) butternut squash, peeled and chopped
100g (4oz) sweet potato, peeled and chopped
Sunflower oil, for cooking
1–2 tsp fresh thyme leaves
1 ripe pear, peeled, cored and chopped

✶ Pre-heat the oven to 200C / 400F / Gas 6.

✶ Put the butternut squash and sweet potatoes into a baking tray lined with foil and brush with sunflower oil. Scatter over the thyme. Cover with a second piece of foil and scrunch the edges together to form a parcel. Bake for about 30 minutes or until tender. Add the pear and blend.

Suitable for freezing
Suitable from 6 months
Makes 2-3 portions

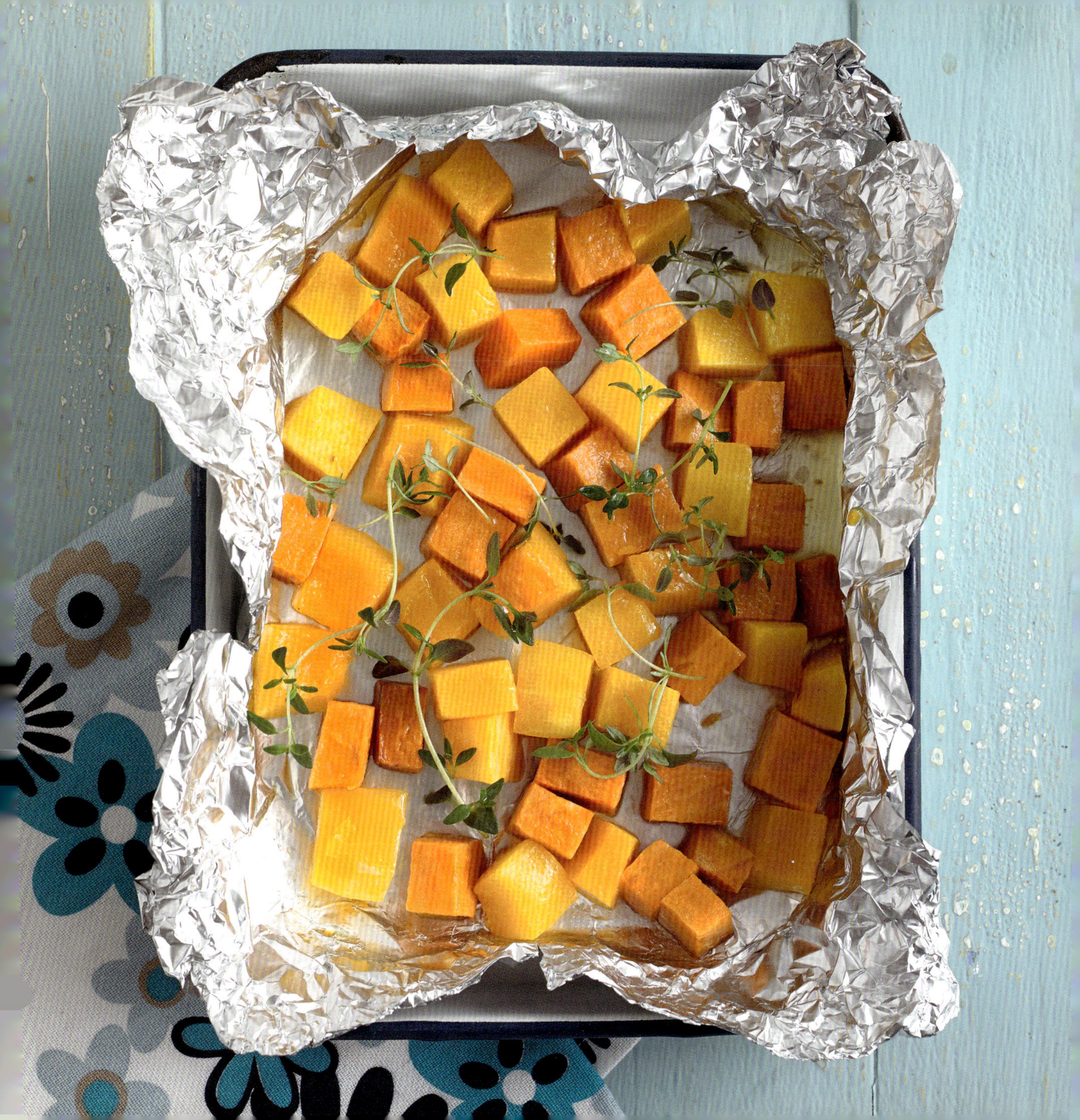

Suitable for freezing
Suitable from 6 months
Makes 4 portions

Butternut squash, spinach and peas

Mixing spinach with sweet-tasting vegetables like butternut squash and peas makes a nice combination. Always wash fresh spinach very carefully to remove all the grit on the leaves. If you prefer, you can leave out the potato and just add extra butternut squash.

Ingredients

300g (10oz) butternut squash, peeled and chopped
1 potato (approx 115g/4oz), peeled and chopped
30g (1oz) baby spinach leaves, washed and drained
20g (1oz) frozen peas

★ Put the butternut squash and potato into a steamer. Cover and cook for 10 minutes. Then add the spinach and peas and continue to cook for 3 minutes. Blend to a purée using an electric hand blender.

Suitable for freezing
Suitable from 6 months
Makes 4 portions

Butternut squash, parsnip, apple and prune

Prunes are a tasty addition to this purée, and will help with constipation. You can also simply cook chopped apples and some chopped prunes in water for a delicious fruit purée that is rich in vitamins A and C and is a good source of fibre.

Ingredients

300g (10oz) butternut squash, peeled and chopped
1 small parsnip (60g/2½oz), peeled and chopped
1 small dessert apple, peeled, cored and chopped
20g (1oz) ready-to-eat prunes
300ml (10fl oz) boiling water

★ Put the butternut squash, parsnip, apple and prunes into a saucepan. Pour over the boiling water, cover and simmer for about 12 minutes or until the vegetables are tender. Purée until smooth using an electric hand blender.

Suitable for freezing
Suitable from 6 months
Makes 2 portions

Parsnip and apple

Parsnip and apple is a popular combination with babies; the fruit emphasises the sweetness of the vegetable.

Ingredients

1 small parsnip (75g/3oz), peeled and sliced
2 dessert apples, peeled, cored and chopped

✶ Put the parsnip into a saucepan and pour over 100ml (3½fl oz) boiling water. Bring to the boil, then reduce the heat, cover and cook for 5 minutes. Add the chopped apple and continue to cook for a further 5 minutes. Blend to a purée.

Suitable for freezing
Suitable from 6 months
Makes 3 portions

Parsnip, pear and swede

Adding fresh pear to the parsnip and swede brings out the natural sweetness of these root vegetables and gives it a smoother texture.

Ingredients

1 small parsnip (60g/2½oz), peeled and chopped
300g (10oz) swede, peeled and chopped
1 ripe pear, peeled, cored and chopped

✶ Put the parsnip and swede into a steamer, cover and cook for 7 minutes. Add the pear and continue to cook for 3 minutes. Blend to a purée.

Carrot, parsnip and apple

Parsnips are easy to digest and unlikely to cause an allergic reaction. They have a sweet nutty flavour that babies love. You can also roast the carrots and parsnip (halve the parsnip and quarter medium-sized carrots) brush with a little olive oil and bake at 200C / 400F / Gas 6 for about 30 minutes until softened, then blend with a little apple purée.

Ingredients

225g (8oz) carrots, peeled and sliced
75g (3oz) parsnips, peeled and sliced
1 dessert apple, peeled, cored and chopped

✶ Put the carrots and parsnips into a steamer, cover and cook for 6 minutes. Add the apple and cook for another 7 minutes. Transfer to a bowl, add a little water from the bottom of the steamer, and blend to a smooth purée using an electric hand blender.

Suitable for freezing
Suitable from 6 months
Makes 4 portions

Carrot and apple

Carrots with their rich orange colour contain more betacarotene than those with a lighter colour. Don't use old and bendy, rubbery carrots with cracked skins; a top tip is to wrap carrots in kitchen towel and store them in the coolest part of the fridge, that way they should keep for up to 2 weeks. If you buy carrots with the leaves attached, cut them off or they wilt and the moisture from the leaves will affect the freshness of the carrots.

Ingredients

225g (8oz) carrots, peeled and sliced
1 dessert apple, peeled, cored and chopped

✶ Put the carrots into a steamer, cover and cook for 6 minutes. Add the apple and continue to cook for another 7 minutes. Transfer to a bowl, add a little water from the bottom of the steamer, and blend using an electric hand blender to make a smooth purée.

Suitable for freezing
Suitable from 6 months
Makes 3 portions

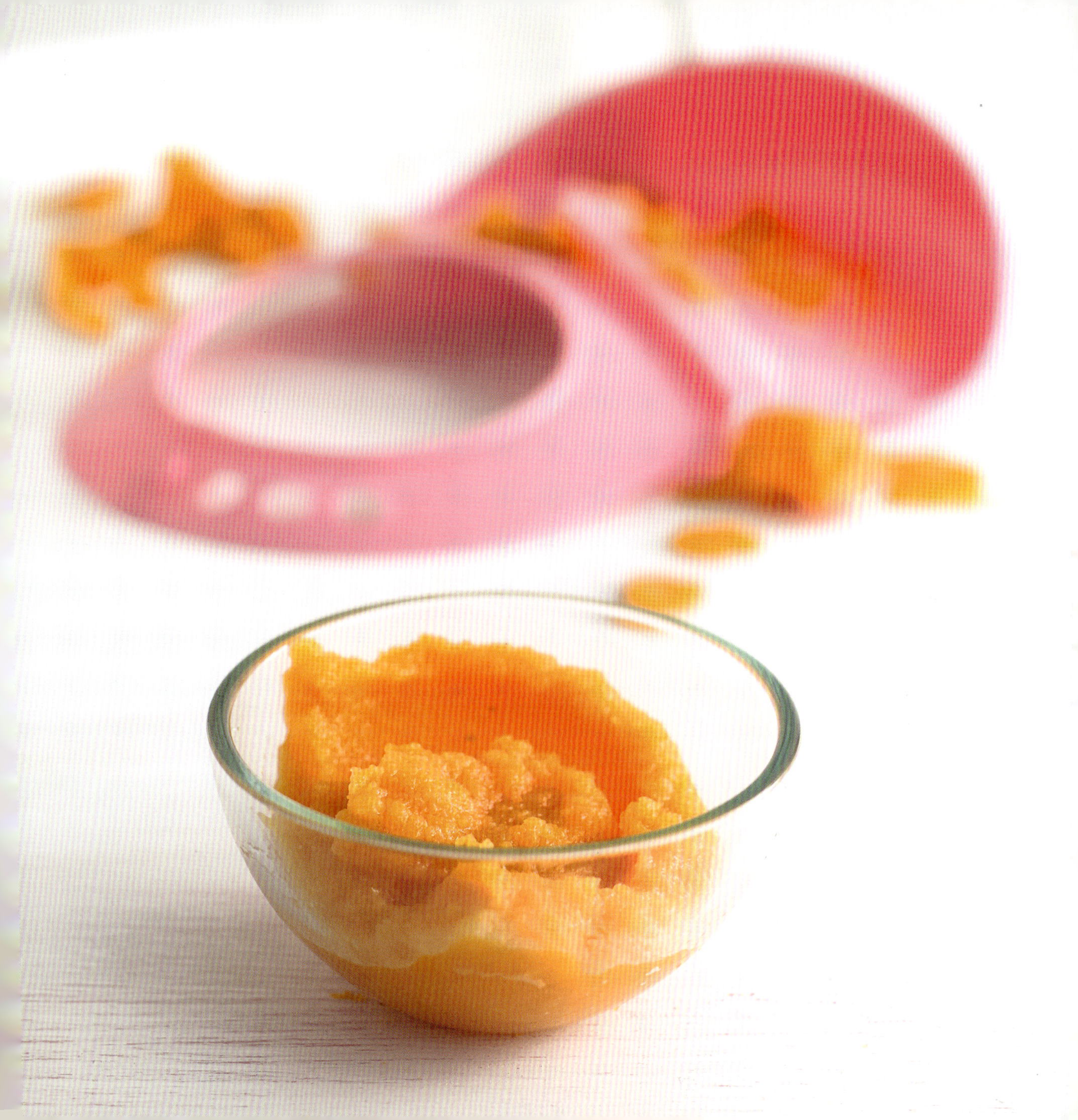

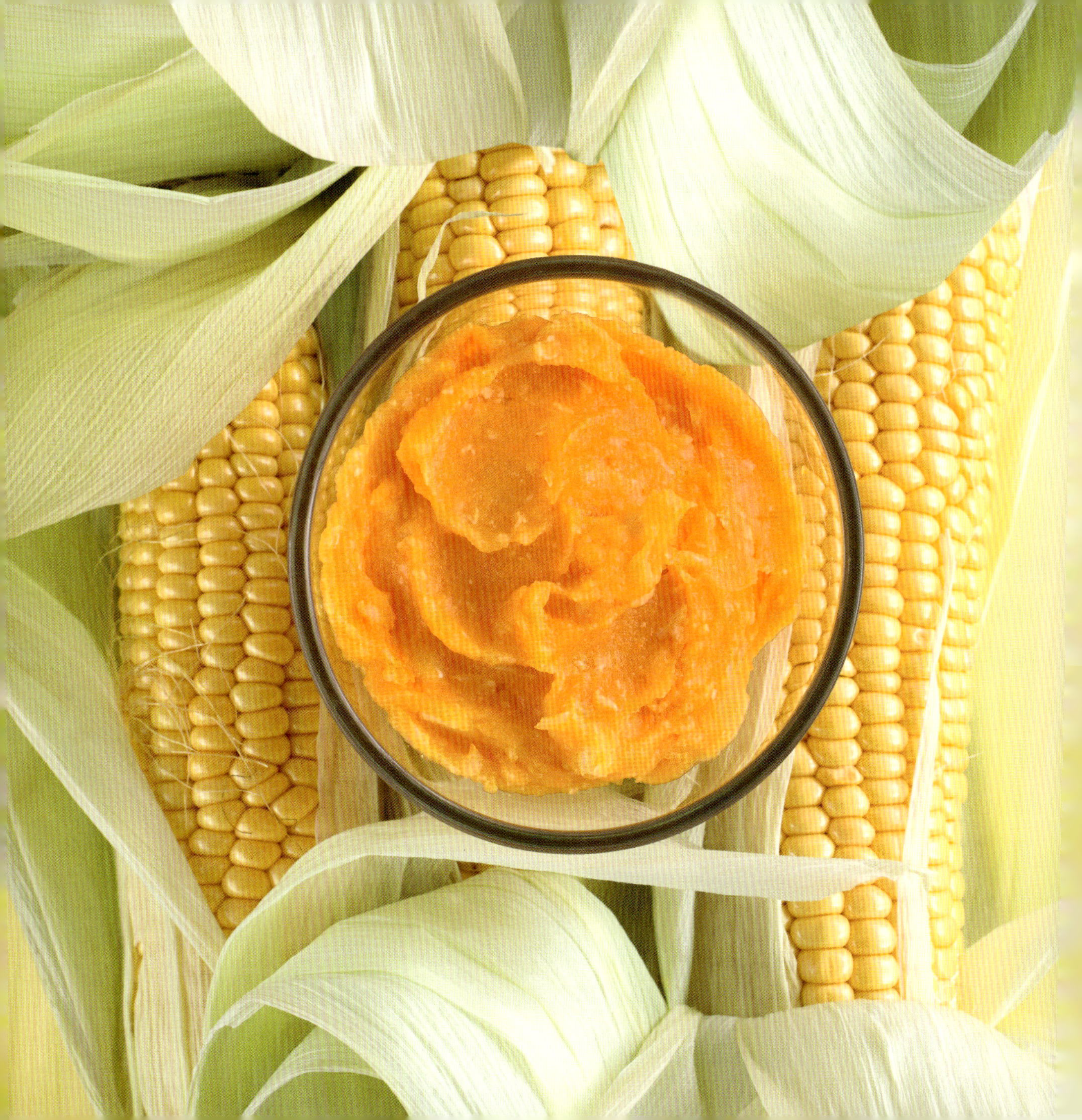

Butternut squash, carrot and sweetcorn

It should be safe to introduce corn to your baby at 6 months, however only give a small amount mixed with other vegetables as it is high in fibre. Occasionally babies who have a family history of allergy or who suffer from eczema may have a reaction to corn.

Ingredients

300g (10oz) butternut squash, peeled and chopped
1 medium carrot (approx 75g/3oz), peeled and sliced
40g (1½oz) sweetcorn, frozen or tinned

✱ Put the butternut squash and carrot into a saucepan and cover with 150ml (5fl oz) boiling water. Cover and cook for 10 minutes. Add the sweetcorn and continue to cook for 3 minutes until all the vegetables are tender. Blend to a purée using an electric hand blender.

Suitable for freezing
Suitable from 6 months
Makes 4 portions

Carrot, potato and sweetcorn

Sweetcorn is best mixed with root vegetables. This recipe is a little like a baby's version of chowder, so you could add a little of your baby's usual milk.

Ingredients

2 carrots, peeled and sliced
1 potato, peeled and chopped
60g (2½oz) sweetcorn, frozen or tinned

✱ Put the carrots and potato into a saucepan and just cover with cold water. Bring to the boil, cover and simmer for 10 minutes. Add the sweetcorn and continue to cook for 4 minutes until all the vegetables are soft. Blend to a purée using an electric hand blender.

Suitable for freezing
Suitable from 6 months
Makes 3 portions

Suitable for freezing
Suitable from 6 months
Makes 4 portions

Sweet potato, broccoli and peas

This makes a good introduction to broccoli, which is one of the most nutritious vegetables you will ever encounter and will help boost your baby's immune system.

Ingredients

1 medium sweet potato, peeled and chopped
1 large potato, peeled and chopped
60g (2½oz) broccoli florets
60g (2½oz) frozen peas

✶ Put the sweet potato and potato into a saucepan, cover with boiling water, bring to the boil, then cover with a lid and simmer for 6 minutes. Add the broccoli and cook for 3 minutes, then add the peas and cook for about another 2–3 minutes. Blend using an electric hand blender.

Suitable for freezing
Suitable from 6 months
Makes 4 portions

Carrot, sweet potato and broccoli

Broccoli is a true superfood. It's an excellent source of vitamins C, A and B and also calcium and folate. Research shows that eating broccoli can help protect you from heart disease and cancer. The best way to introduce broccoli to your baby is combined with root vegetables.

Ingredients

250g (9oz) carrots, peeled and chopped
250g (9oz) sweet potatoes, peeled and chopped
75g (3oz) broccoli florets

✶ Put the carrots and sweet potato into a steamer, cover and cook for 12 minutes. Add the broccoli and continue to cook for 5 minutes or until all the vegetables are tender. Purée using an electric hand blender, adding a little of the water from the bottom of the steamer to make a smooth purée.

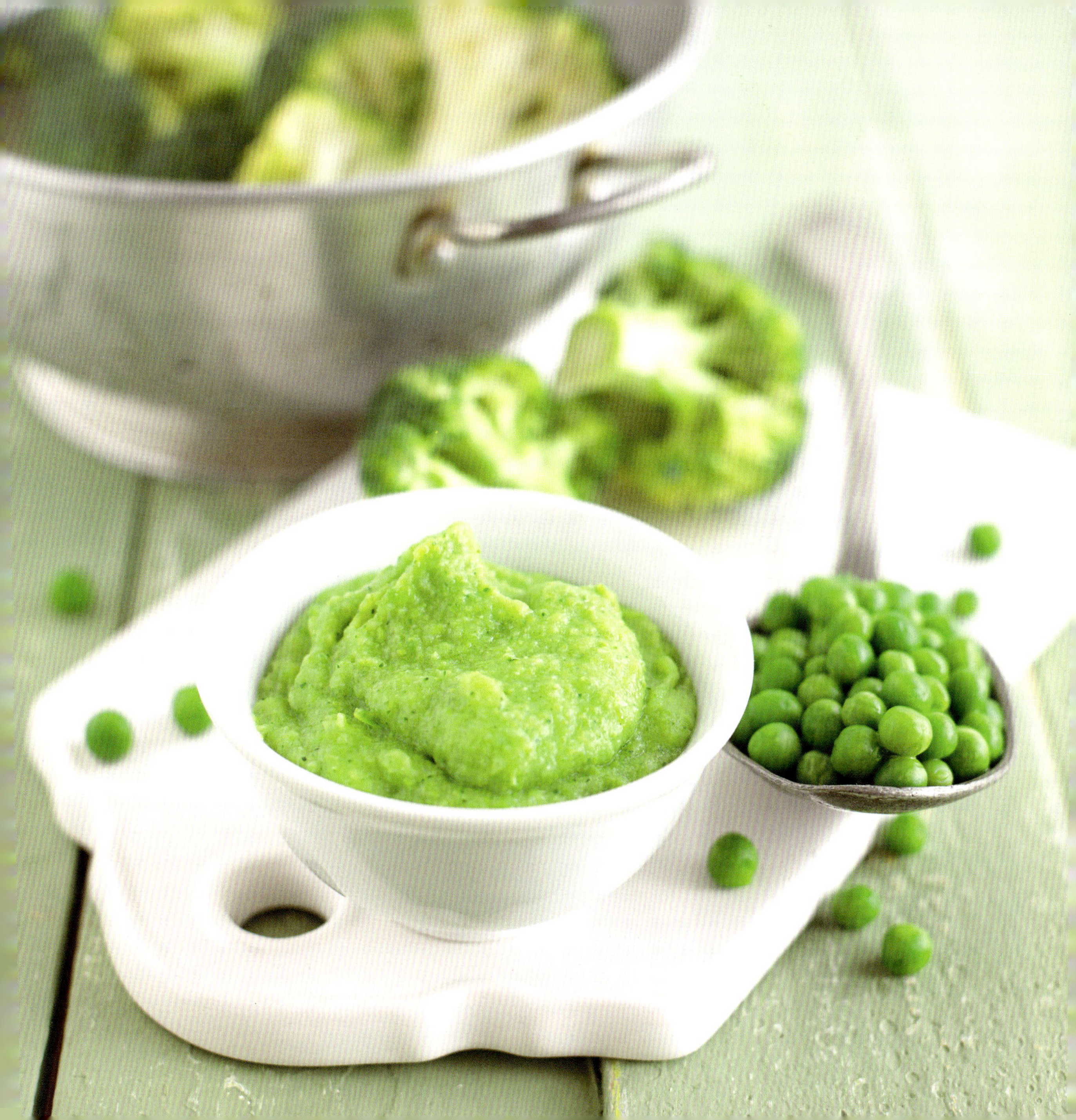

6 to 9 months

Exploring new tastes and textures

Between the ages of 6 and 9 months, your baby will do a lot of developing, making feeding easier for them and for you. A 7-month-old will still need supporting whilst you are feeding him, however a 9-month-old baby is usually strong enough to sit in a high chair whilst he is being fed, and may have more teeth to chew with. Although, if your baby still has very few teeth, don't worry, as they do not need to have teeth to learn to chew, you will be surprised at what strong gums can get through!

At this stage of weaning, you can become more adventurous and introduce new foods such as meat, fish and eggs, lentils and small pasta shapes. Purées can be thicker, and you can add tiny lumps and mashed or finely minced foods. For young babies choose foods that are soft and can melt in the mouth, particularly when introducing finger foods. Don't give young babies chunks of meat, cheese, whole grapes or raw vegetables, as they could choke on them. Never leave a baby unattended with finger food, in case they choke (see page 98 for tips on how to deal with choking), let them experiment with picking up food and try not to help them too much, but always stay in the same room.

Learning to chew

It is very common for babies to have problems eating lumpy food. Those babies who are only fed on jars in particular find it very difficult to move on to large lumps such as chunks of meat. It is therefore important to introduce texture and small lumps in their food as early as possible, because the older they are, the more reluctant they will be to eat it. Lumpy food will encourage them to use muscles as they chew, and these same muscles are also used for speech.

Try thickening purées first, then add lumps. Adding lumps consistently throughout the food is better than your baby finding a surprise one, so try adding tiny pasta shapes, rice or couscous. Well-cooked scrambled eggs are another good way of introducing texture.

Foods for little fingers

Offering soft finger foods from 7 months is a good idea as many babies learn to eat lumps this way rather than in purées. Fingers of toasted bread, lightly steamed vegetable sticks, chunks of banana, tiny pieces of cheese, grated apple and rice cakes make good finger foods.

Introducing fish, chicken, beef and eggs

From 6 months old your baby can eat protein, so it is a good idea to introduce foods like eggs, cheese, pulses, chicken and fish now. At this stage your baby needs nutrient-dense meals; giving only fruit and vegetables that are low in calories is not enough. Babies grow more rapidly in the first year than at any other time in their life. Babies need calories to grow as well as nutrients that proteins provide.

Chicken

Chicken is an ideal first meat. It's very versatile and combines well with root vegetables like carrot or sweet potato, which give it a smoother texture. Chicken also combines well with fruits like apple, apricot or grapes. As well as chicken breast, try using the thigh meat – this dark meat contains twice as much iron as the white and is less expensive than breast meat too.

Meat

Red meat, such as beef, is one of the best, most easily absorbable sources of iron. Babies often reject red meat because of its chewy texture, though, so it is a good idea to combine it with root vegetables and slow-cook the meat to produce a smoother texture that is easier to swallow. Iron is vitally important for your baby's brain development. The iron your baby inherits from his mother starts to run out at around 6 months, so this is when you need to make sure you are including iron-rich foods in your baby's diet.

Fish

Try mixing fish with stronger tastes such as carrots, tomato and grated Cheddar. If fish is overcooked it becomes tough and tasteless; it is cooked when it just flakes with a fork but is still firm. Always check very carefully for bones before serving. Oily fish such as salmon or mackerel is a great source of omega 3 fats, which are vital for your baby's brain development, nervous system and vision.

Fruit and vegetables

Your baby should now be able to eat all fruit and vegetables. You can simply combine different vegetables to ring the changes, or mix more bitter vegetables such as spinach with sweet root vegetables or add cheese sauce to make them more appealing to your baby. Fruit and vegetables make good first soft finger foods – particularly steamed vegetables, like carrot sticks or small florets of cauliflower – and both fresh and dried fruit make good snacks.

Cereals

Your baby can now have some 'adult' cereals like Weetabix, porridge and Ready Brek. At this age you can mix cereals with cow's milk, if you wish.

Pasta

Try cooking small pasta shapes like mini shells, stars and alphabet letters and stirring them into your baby's purées so that they learn to chew.

Pulses

Lentils and other dried peas and beans are great for all babies and especially important for those who are being brought up on a vegetarian diet. Lentils are a good source of protein, iron and fibre. Lentils and beans can be indigestible to young babies, though, so you may need to limit how much you give them.

Nuts

If there is no family history of allergy (see pages 10–12), very finely ground nuts can be a useful weaning food. They are very nutritious and are a good source of protein, particularly for vegetarian babies. However, watch out for the salt and sugar content in some products.

If you have a family history of allergy you should speak to your GP or health visitor before introducing any peanut products.

Children under 5 should not be given any whole nuts because of the risk of choking.

Dairy products

It's fine to include cow's milk in cooking or with your baby's cereal, but do not introduce it as a main drink for your baby yet as it is not rich enough in certain vitamins and minerals. Cheese, yogurt and fromage frais can now be included in your baby's diet, though. Babies grow at a rapid rate in the first year so you should always give them full-fat milk and dairy products. Always choose pasteurised cheese and avoid blue cheeses, Brie, Camembert and feta cheese until your baby is at least 12 months old. Watch out for the high sugar content in some processed yogurts and fromage frais.

Finger foods

Many babies are determined to feed themselves, however at 6 months their hand-to-eye coordination isn't sufficiently developed for them to feed themselves successfully enough to get all the nutrients they need. However, it is important to give your baby a selection of soft finger foods to experiment with alongside purées. The more opportunities babies get to feed themselves, the quicker they will master the art. Here are some foods to try:

- ✱ Soft ripe fruits, eg: pear, mango, banana, peach
- ✱ Dried fruit eg: dried apricot or apple
- ✱ Steamed vegetables eg: carrot sticks or broccoli florets
- ✱ Fingers of toast
- ✱ Cooked pasta shapes
- ✱ Rice cakes
- ✱ Pieces of chicken or fish or wafer-thin cooked meats, rolled up
- ✱ Sticks or slices of cheese

Drinks

Once your baby is 7–8 months old you can start cutting down on their milk feeds so that they are hungrier for solids. However, they still need 500–600ml breast or formula milk per day. You can also offer water or diluted fruit juice with meals if your baby seems thirsty. Only put formula, breast milk or water into your baby's bottle; sucking on sweet or fruit drinks is the main cause of tooth decay in young children.

Vegetarian diet

If you decide you would like your baby to follow a vegetarian diet, be aware that it needs to be carefully balanced and should not contain too much fibre. A high-fibre diet, whilst fine for adults, is too low in calories and essential fats for babies and hinders their absorption of iron. You will need to ensure they are getting enough protein, iron, zinc and B vitamins too, so make sure you include the following foods in their diet: dairy products, eggs, beans and pulses (such as lentils), green leafy vegetables (such as broccoli, spinach) and fortified breakfast cereals.

Baby's appetite

Let your baby's appetite determine how much they eat and never force them to eat something they dislike. If they refuse something, don't offer it for a while, but reintroduce it a few weeks later. Remember, at this age it is normal for babies to be quite chubby – as soon as your baby starts crawling and walking, they will lose any excess weight.

It is very difficult to recommend specific portion sizes, as the quantity that individual babies eat varies enormously. Babies have different metabolic rates and different activity levels, and the amount they eat can also vary from week to week. However, by 7 months old, babies should ideally be having three solid meals a day, supplemented with their usual milk (see page 9).

6–9 months meal planner

	Breakfast	Mid-morning	Lunch	Mid-afternoon	Tea	Bedtime
Day 1	Porridge with apple, pear & yogurt Milk	Milk	Chicken, pear, parsnip & carrot Water or juice Blueberry, pear & banana	Milk	Mediterranean vegetable purée Apple & nectarine Water or juice	Milk
Day 2	Weetabix with milk Mashed banana Milk	Milk	Salmon with carrot & orange Apple & nectarine Water or juice	Milk	Lentil purée with tomato & cheese Mashed banana Water or juice Blueberry, pear & banana	Milk
Day 3	Porridge, apricot & banana Milk	Milk	Carrot, apple & spinach purée Yogurt Water or juice	Milk	My first beef bolognese Rusk Water or juice	Milk
Day 4	Apple purée & baby cereal Toast Milk	Milk	Chicken, apricot & butternut squash Fruit Water or juice	Milk	Cauliflower, spinach & courgette Yogurt & mashed banana Water or juice	Milk
Day 5	Porridge with milk Fruit purée Milk	Milk	Lentil purée Fruit Water or juice	Milk	Tasty beef casserole Yogurt Water or juice	Milk
Day 6	Baby cereal with milk Apricot & pear purée Milk	Milk	Sweet potato, Pea & leek Blueberry, pear & banana Water or juice	Milk	Salmon with sweet potato, tomato and basil Fruit Water or juice	Milk
Day 7	Weetabix with milk Apricot & pear purée Milk	Milk	Butternut squash, tomato & pepper Rusk Water or juice	Milk	Chicken, squash & spinach purée Pear purée Water or juice	Milk

Vegetables

Suitable for freezing
Suitable from 6 months
Makes 4 portions

Butternut squash, tomato and pepper

Ingredients

200g (7oz) butternut squash, peeled and chopped
75g (3oz) red pepper, deseeded and diced
120g (4½oz) courgette, diced
40g (1½oz) dessert apple, peeled, cored and diced
½ x 400g can chopped tomatoes
300ml (10fl oz) unsalted vegetable stock
25g (1oz) Cheddar cheese, grated

A delicious trio of flavours to tickle your baby's tastebuds. You can save yourself time by buying butternut squash that is already peeled and chopped.

★ Put the squash, pepper, courgette, apple, tomatoes and stock into a saucepan. Bring up to the boil, cover and simmer for 15 minutes until tender. Blend until smooth, then add the cheese and stir until melted.

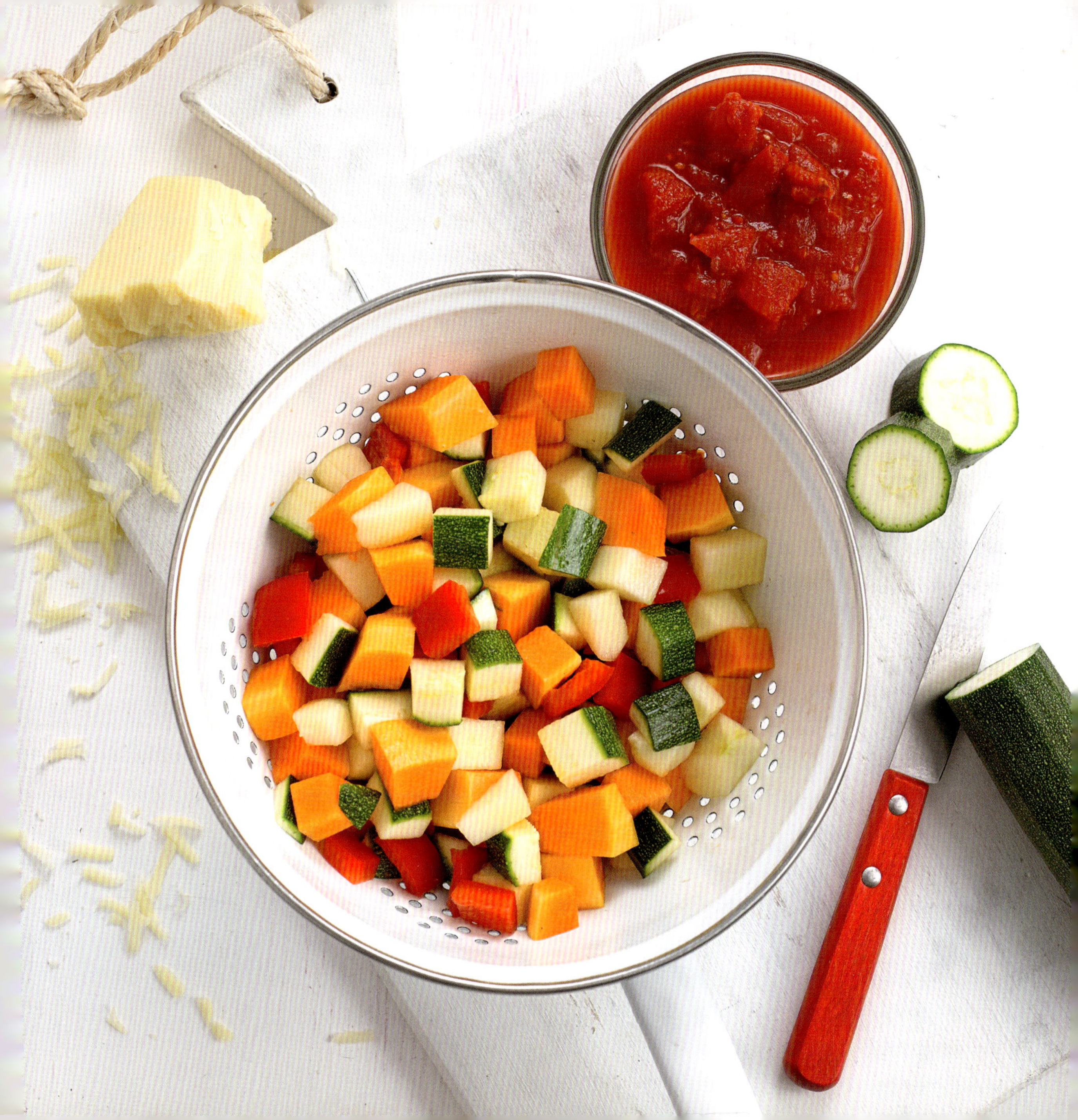

Suitable for freezing
Suitable from 6 months
Makes 5 portions

Swede, parsnip and broccoli

Broccoli is very high in vitamin C and is a great source of soluble fibre. Mixing it with sweet root vegetables is a wonderful way to introduce this powerful veggie.

Ingredients

350g (12oz) swede, peeled and diced
200g (7oz) parsnips, peeled and diced
500ml (18fl oz) unsalted vegetable stock
75g (3oz) small broccoli florets

✱ Put the swede, parsnip and stock in a saucepan. Bring up to the boil, cover with a lid and simmer for 15 minutes. Add the broccoli and simmer for another 5 minutes until tender. Blend until smooth.

Suitable for freezing
Suitable from 6 months
Makes 5 portions

Mediterranean vegetable purée

This lovely Mediterranean medley of vegetables is full of goodness for your baby. Serve it on its own or mix it with a little couscous for added texture.

Ingredients

100g (4oz) red onion, peeled and chopped
150g (5oz) courgette, diced
100g (4oz) yellow pepper, deseeded and diced
175g (6oz) aubergine, diced
1 clove garlic, crushed
400g can chopped tomatoes
200ml (7fl oz) unsalted vegetable stock
1 tbsp tomato purée
1 tbsp chopped fresh basil
30g (1oz) Cheddar cheese, grated

✱ Put all of the ingredients except the basil and cheese into a saucepan. Cover with a lid, bring up to the boil, then simmer for 15 minutes until all the vegetables are soft. Add the basil then blend everything until smooth. Stir in the cheese until it is all melted.

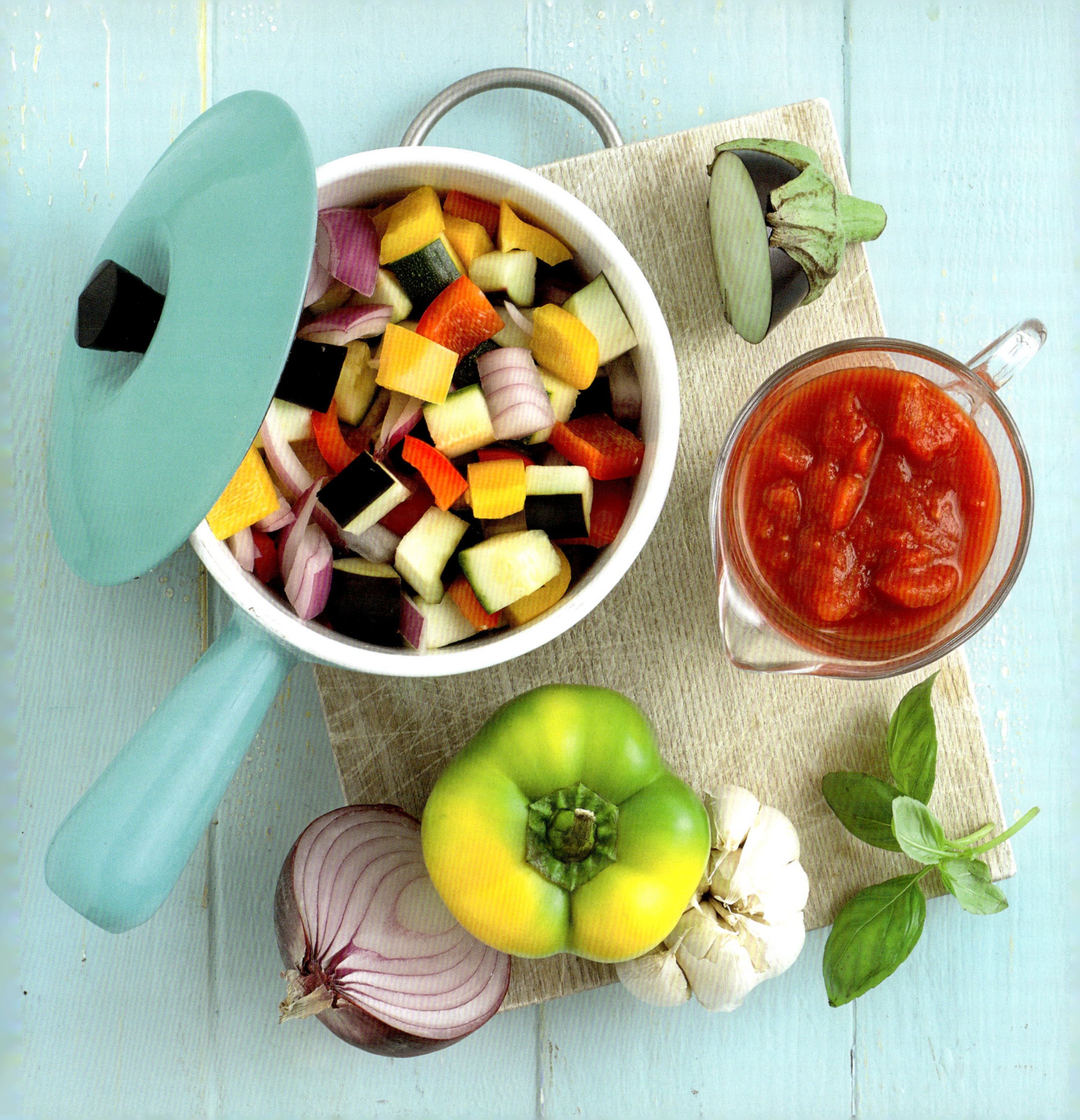

Suitable for freezing
Suitable from 6 months
Makes 3 portions

Lentil purée

Ingredients

2 tsp olive oil
50g (2oz) red onion, peeled and diced
50g (2oz) red pepper, deseeded and diced
50g (2oz) courgette, diced
2 medium carrots, peeled and chopped
1 clove garlic, crushed
3 tbsp red lentils
¼ tsp ground coriander
½ x 400g can chopped tomatoes
200ml (7fl oz) unsalted chicken stock
1 tsp sundried tomato paste
2 tsp chopped fresh basil
15g (½oz) Parmesan, grated

You might not have thought of giving your baby lentils, but some of my most popular baby recipes are made with these pulses. Lentils are a good source of protein, iron and fibre; and one of the reasons why we introduce solids at six months is because the iron a baby inherits from his or her mother runs out at this age, so it's important to provide it through their food.

✶ Heat the oil in a saucepan. Add the onion, pepper, courgette and carrots and fry for 5 minutes. Add the garlic and fry for 1 minute. Add the lentils and coriander, then stir in the tomatoes, stock and tomato paste. Bring up to the boil, cover with a lid and simmer for 20 minutes. Blend until smooth using an electric hand blender. Add the basil and Parmesan just before serving.

Carrot, apple and spinach purée

Suitable for freezing
Suitable from 6 months
Makes 2 portions

A good way to introduce new vegetables is to mix them up with familiar ones. Interestingly, sautéing carrots in a little olive oil makes it easier for your baby to absorb their beneficial betacarotene.

✶ Heat the oil in a large saucepan and sauté the carrots for 5–6 minutes until starting to soften.

✶ Add the apples and about 50ml (2fl oz) water and bring up to the boil. Simmer for 8–10 minutes until the carrots and apples are soft and the water has evaporated.

✶ Add the spinach leaves and 2 tablespoons water and cook, stirring, until the spinach has wilted and the water has evaporated.

✶ Leave to cool and then purée. If a smoother texture is needed you can blend the vegetables with 2–3 tablespoons of your baby's usual milk.

Ingredients

1 tbsp olive oil
2 medium carrots, peeled and chopped
2 medium dessert apples, peeled, cored and chopped
2 large handfuls of baby spinach leaves, washed and drained, larger stalks removed
2–3 tbsp of your baby's usual milk (optional)

Butternut squash, carrot and broccoli

Your baby now needs proportionately more fat in their diet than adults; mixing vegetables with cheese is a good way to make a more nutrient-dense meal.

Ingredients

100g (4oz) butternut squash, peeled and diced
100g (4oz) carrots, peeled and diced
120g (4½oz) broccoli florets
250ml (9fl oz) unsalted vegetable stock
1 tsp cream cheese
20g (1oz) Cheddar cheese, grated

✱ Put the squash, carrots, broccoli and stock into a saucepan. Bring up to the boil then simmer for 15 minutes until tender. Blend to a chunky consistency then stir in the cream cheese and Cheddar.

Suitable for freezing
Suitable from 6 months
Makes 3 portions

Cauliflower, spinach and courgette

Filled with essential vitamins and minerals, these vegetables are some of the most nutrient-dense around. When cooked properly, they can also be some of the most delicious.

Ingredients

A knob of butter
100g (4oz) cauliflower florets
1 onion, peeled and chopped
1 courgette, diced
1 tomato, quartered
150ml (5fl oz) unsalted vegetable stock
30g (1oz) spinach leaves, washed, drained and chopped
2 tbsp grated Parmesan

✱ Heat the butter in a saucepan. Add the cauliflower, onion, courgette and tomato and cook for 2 minutes, stirring occasionally. Add the stock, then simmer for 15 minutes. Add the spinach, then blend until smooth. Finally, stir in the cheese.

Suitable for freezing
Suitable from 6 months
Makes 3 portions

Suitable for freezing
Suitable from 6 months
Makes 3 portions

Parsnip, celeriac and carrot

This is a great way to introduce the new flavour of celeriac to your baby. Although this root veggie is rather ugly and knobbly in appearance, it has a deliciously distinctive flavour. Peel it thickly and cut away the root so you are left with the creamy white flesh.

Ingredients
150g (5oz) parsnips, peeled and diced
150g (5oz) celeriac, peeled and diced
150g (5oz) carrots, peeled and diced
1½ tbsp cream cheese

✱ Put the root vegetables into a saucepan, cover with water and boil for about 15 minutes until tender. Drain the vegetables, then put into a blender and blend until smooth. Stir in the cream cheese.

Suitable for freezing
Suitable from 6 months
Makes 3 portions

Sweet potato, pea and leek

For freshness, great taste and convenience, try using frozen vegetables. They tend to be picked and frozen within hours of harvest which means they retain lots of important nutrients for your baby's development.

Ingredients
A knob of butter
125g (4½oz) leeks, trimmed, washed and chopped
175g (6oz) sweet potatoes, peeled and diced
400ml (14fl oz) unsalted vegetable stock
100g (4oz) frozen peas

✱ Melt the butter in a saucepan. Add the leeks and sweet potato and toss them in the butter. Pour in the stock, bring up to the boil, then cover with a lid and simmer for 15 minutes. Add the peas 5 minutes before the end of the cooking time. Drain all the vegetables and blend together until smooth using an electric hand blender.

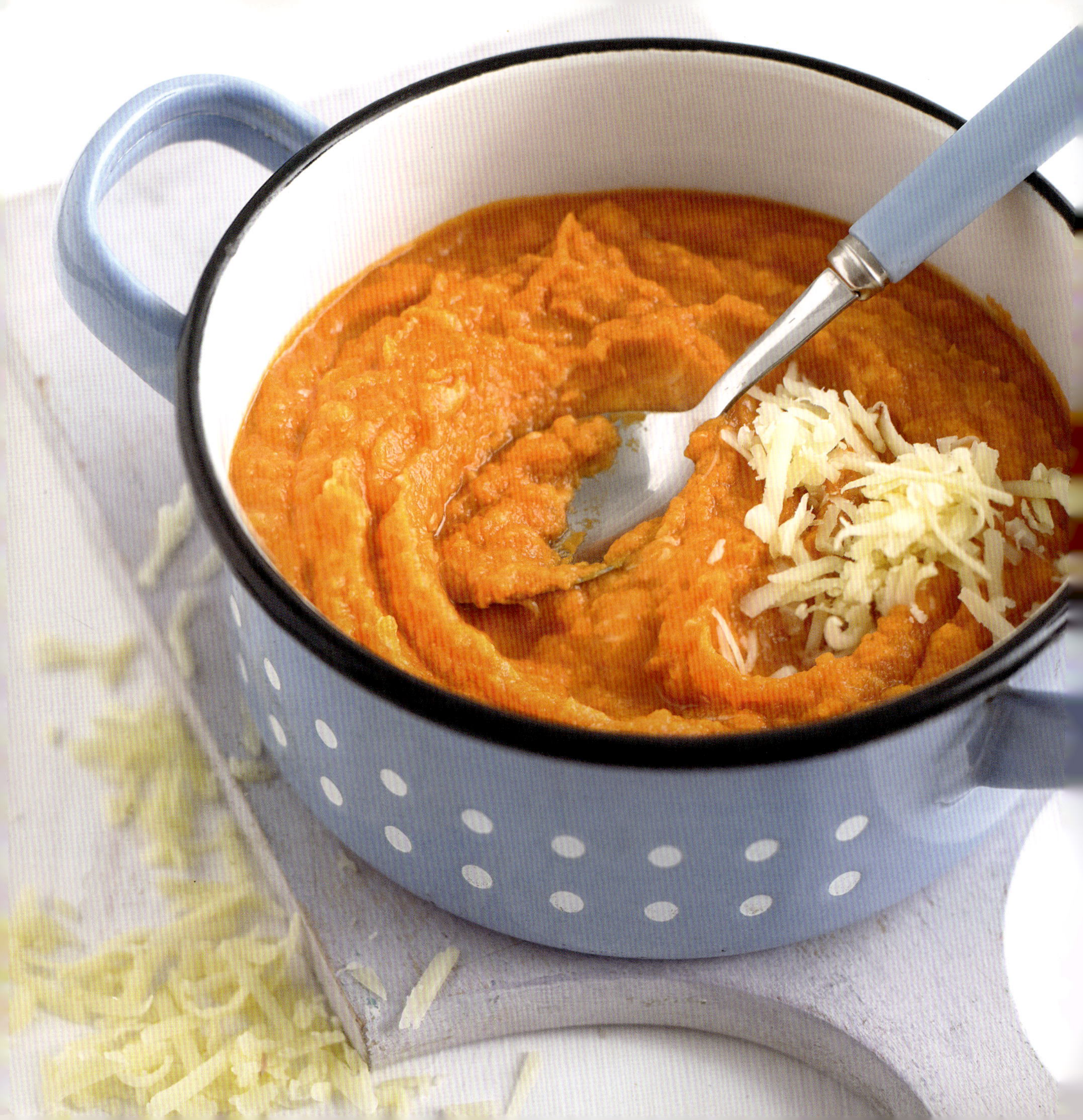

Lentil purée with tomato and cheese

Suitable for freezing
Suitable from 6 months
Makes 6 portions

This lovely lentil recipe makes a sweet, soft purée that your baby will love at this stage. Lentils are a good source of protein, iron and fibre – all of which are important for your baby's development. A quick tip; red lentils are best for purées as they cook faster and are smoother than other types of lentils.

✶ Heat the vegetable oil in a saucepan and sauté the onion, carrots, celery and garlic for 5 minutes. Tip the lentils into a sieve and rinse under running water, drain, then add to the pan. Add the sweet potato and sauté for 1 minute. Pour in the passata and water, then cover and cook for about 30 minutes. Remove from the heat and stir in the cheese until melted. Blend until smooth.

Ingredients

1 tbsp vegetable oil
1 small onion, peeled and chopped
100g (4oz) carrots, peeled and chopped
15g (½oz) celery, chopped
1 small clove garlic, crushed
50g (2oz) split red lentils
250g (9oz) sweet potatoes, peeled and chopped
200g (7oz) tomato passata
200ml (7fl oz) water
40g (1½oz) mature Cheddar cheese, grated

Suitable for freezing
Suitable from 6 months
Makes 3 portions

Salmon with carrot and orange

Ingredients

A knob of butter
200g (7oz) carrots, peeled and diced
180g (6oz) tomatoes, deseeded and chopped
25g (1oz) orange peeled, white pith removed, and chopped
300ml (10fl oz) unsalted vegetable stock
100g (4oz) boneless, skinless salmon fillet
15g (½oz) Cheddar cheese, grated

The essential fatty acids in oily fish such as salmon are extremely important for the development of your baby's brain, nervous system and vision, so it helps to introduce it in a way that your baby will love. Orange is my secret ingredient; it's high in vitamin C and will add a tasty zing.

✲ Melt the butter in a saucepan. Add the carrots and tomatoes and coat in the butter. Add the orange and stock and bring everything up to the boil, then cover and simmer for 15 minutes until tender. Add the salmon after 10 minutes and cook through. Blend until smooth or mash for older babies. Stir in the cheese until melted.

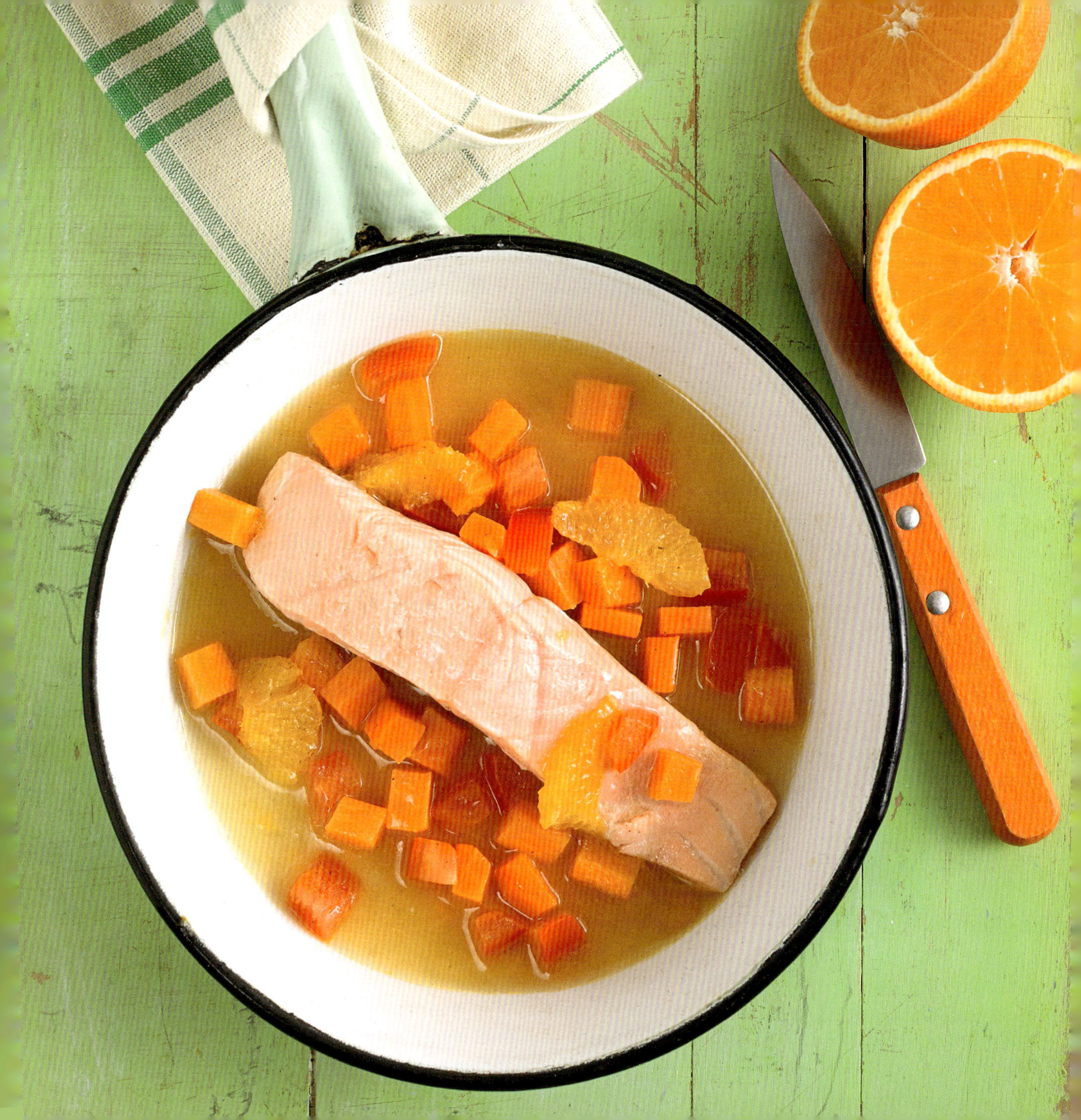

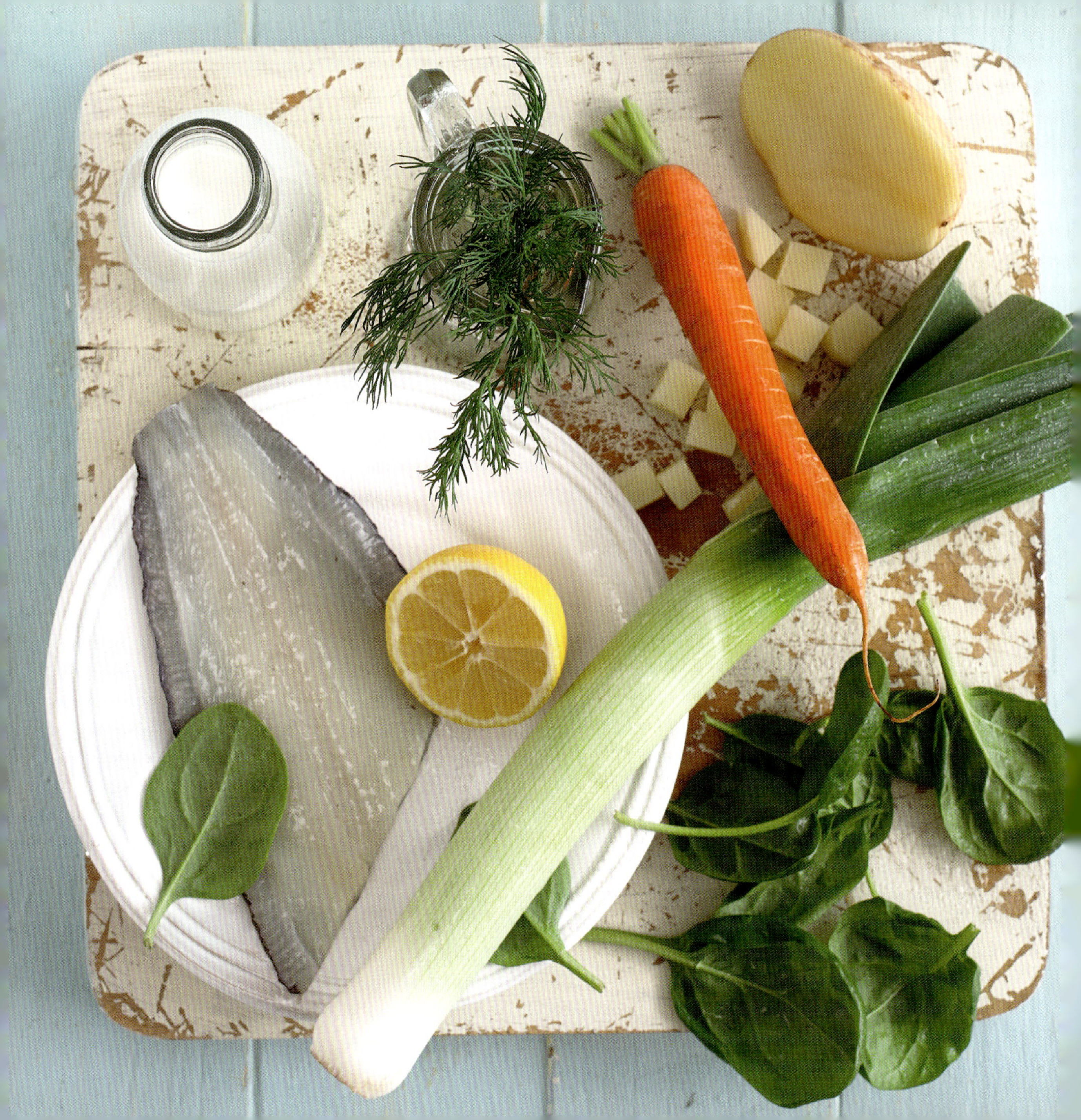

Lemon sole and spinach purée

Suitable for freezing
Suitable from 6 months
Makes 5 portions

It's so easy to cook fish in a microwave; it only takes a few minutes. Fresh dill adds a delicious flavour to this purée.

* Melt the butter in a saucepan. Add the leek, carrots and potatoes and stir for 2 minutes. Add the stock, bring up to the boil, cover with a lid and simmer for 15 minutes until the potatoes are soft.

* Put the milk into a bowl. Add the sole, skin side up, cover the bowl with clingfilm and pierce a few holes in it using a sharp knife. Microwave for 3 minutes on High. Once cool enough to handle, peel the skin from the fish, reserving the cooking milk.

* Add the spinach, dill and lemon juice to the cooked vegetables and stir until the spinach has wilted. Add the milk and sole, then blend everything together until smooth, or mash for older babies. Stir in the cheese until it has melted, if using.

Ingredients

A knob of butter
1 leek, trimmed, washed and roughly chopped
80g (3oz) carrots, peeled and diced
200g (7oz) potatoes, peeled and diced
300ml (10fl oz) unsalted chicken stock
75ml (3fl oz) milk
250g (9oz) boneless lemon sole fillet, skin on
50g (2oz) spinach leaves, washed and drained
2 tsp chopped fresh dill
1 tsp lemon juice
15g (½oz) Parmesan, grated (optional)

Suitable for freezing
Suitable from 6 months
Makes 5 portions

Salmon with sweet potato, tomato and basil

Ingredients

1 tsp olive oil
75g (3oz) red pepper, deseeded and diced
100g (4oz) onion, peeled and diced
200g (7oz) sweet potatoes, peeled and diced
½ x 400g can chopped tomatoes
300ml (10fl oz) water
250g (9oz) boneless, skinless salmon fillet, cut into small cubes
15g (½oz) Cheddar cheese, grated
2 tbsp chopped fresh basil

A very tasty Mediterranean-style salmon purée with tomato, sweet pepper and basil.

✱ Heat the oil in a saucepan. Add the pepper and onion and fry for 2 minutes. Add the potatoes, tomatoes and water, bring up to the boil, cover with a lid and simmer for 15 minutes. Add the salmon and simmer for another 5 minutes until cooked through. Stir in the cheese and basil, then blend until smooth or mash for older babies.

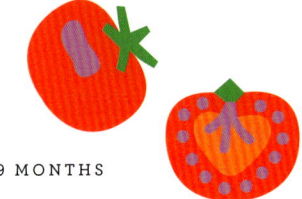

Salmon and dill purée

Suitable for freezing
Suitable from 6 months
Makes approx 3 portions

It's important to introduce oily fish from 6 months. The essential fatty acids they contain are vital for your baby's development. Since you can't add salt to your baby's purées, use fresh herbs for flavour – dill goes really well with fish.

✶ Heat the butter in a saucepan. Add the onion and fry for 2 minutes. Add the potatoes and carrots and fry for 3 minutes. Add the milk, bring up to the boil, cover with a lid and simmer for 15 minutes. Add the dill and the salmon and simmer for 5 minutes until cooked. Blend until smooth using an electric hand blender or mash for older babies. Stir through the lemon juice.

Ingredients

A knob of butter
75g (3oz) onion, peeled and diced
125g (4½oz) sweet potatoes, peeled and diced
75g (3oz) carrots, peeled and diced
250ml (9fl oz) milk
1 tsp chopped fresh dill
100g (4oz) boneless, skinless salmon fillet, cut into cubes
1 tsp lemon juice

6 TO 9 MONTHS

Suitable for freezing
Suitable from 6 months
Makes 4 portions

Plaice with butternut squash

Ingredients

A knob of butter
100g (4oz) leeks, trimmed, washed and chopped
225g (8oz) butternut squash, peeled and diced
200ml (7fl oz) unsalted fish stock
100ml (3½fl oz) milk
350g (12oz) boneless plaice fillets, skin on
1 tsp lemon juice
25g (1oz) Cheddar cheese, grated

Once babies are able to cope with a coarser texture you can mash the recipes with fish rather than purée them.

✷ Melt the butter in a saucepan. Add the leeks and squash and fry for 2 minutes. Add the stock, then simmer for 15 minutes until the vegetables are tender.

✷ Put the milk and plaice into a bowl, cover with clingfilm and pierce a few holes in it using a sharp knife. Cook in the microwave for 3 minutes on High until cooked through.

✷ When cool enough to handle, peel the skin from the fish and put the fish into a bowl, reserving the milk. Add the vegetables to the fish and blend until smooth. Add a little of the reserved cooking milk if the mixture is too thick. Stir in the lemon juice and then the cheese, until melted.

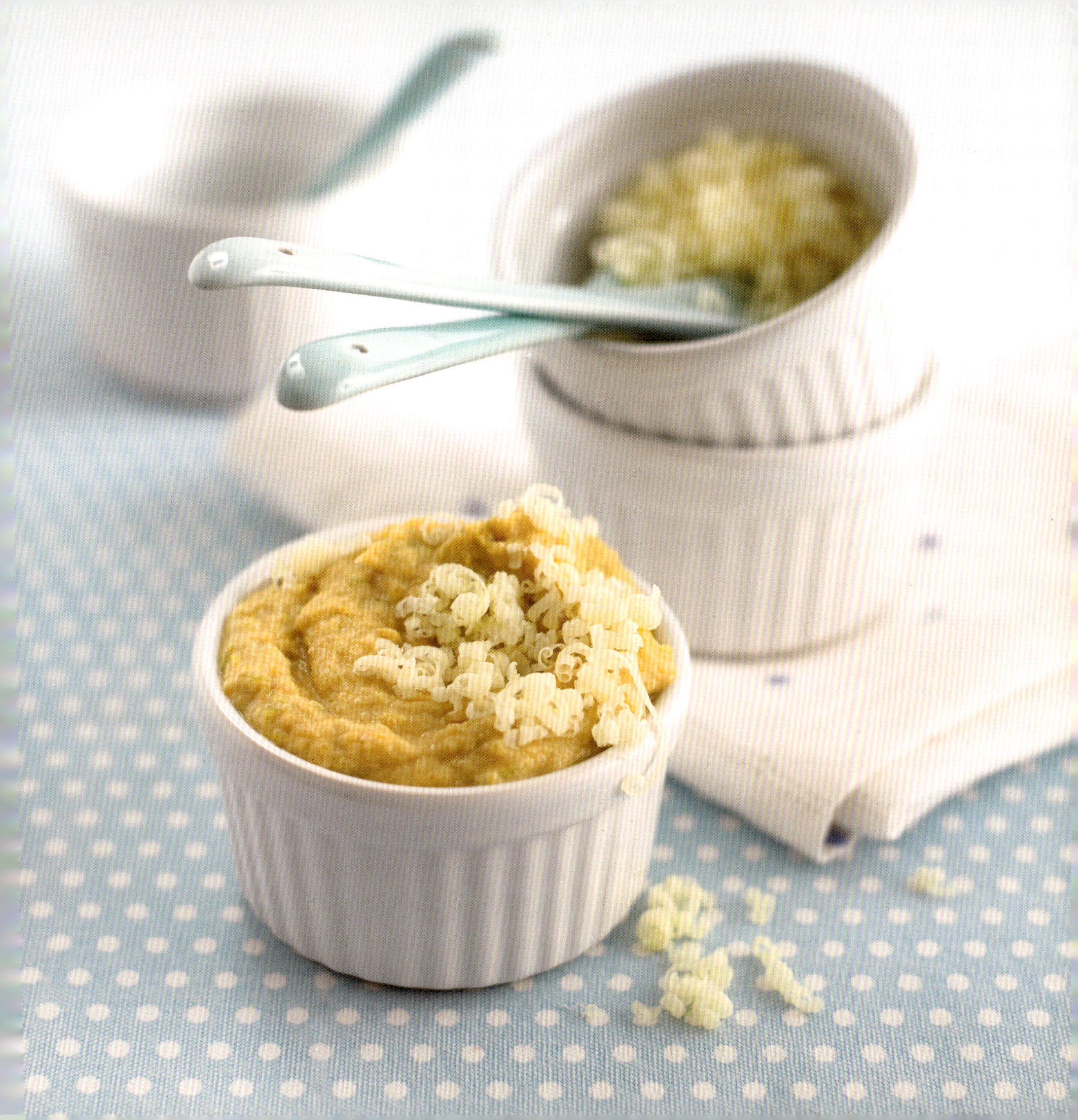

Suitable for freezing
Suitable from 6 months
Makes 3 portions

Cod with sweet potato, celery and carrot

Ingredients

150g (5oz) sweet potatoes, peeled and diced
150g (5oz) carrots, peeled and diced
100g (4oz) celery, diced
100g (4oz) potatoes, peeled and diced
300ml (10fl oz) unsalted vegetable stock
50g (2oz) boneless, skinless cod fillet, cut into small cubes
1 tbsp cream cheese

The vegetable part of this purée is delicious on its own, but the fish and cream cheese add a lovely creaminess to it, and incorporates the fat a baby needs in its diet. This fish recipe is anything but bland!

★ Put the vegetables and stock into a saucepan. Bring up to the boil, cover and simmer for 10 minutes. Add the cod and simmer for another 5 minutes. Blend until smooth or mash for older babies then stir in the cream cheese.

Salmon, courgette and carrot

Suitable for freezing
Suitable from 6 months
Makes 4 portions

So many children grow up only eating fish as fish fingers, so it's important to instill a love of fish itself at an early age.

✱ Melt the butter in a saucepan. Add the onion, carrots and courgettes and fry for 2 minutes. Add the stock, then simmer for 15 minutes until the vegetables are soft. Add the salmon and simmer for 5 minutes. Blend everything together until smooth or mash for older babies. Stir in the Cheddar until melted.

Ingredients

A knob of butter
1 onion, peeled and chopped
140g (5oz) carrots, peeled and diced
125g (4½oz) courgettes, diced
300ml (10fl oz) unsalted fish stock
100g (4oz) boneless, skinless salmon fillet, cut into cubes
30g (1oz) Cheddar cheese, grated

Suitable for freezing
Suitable from 6 months
Makes approx 3 portions

Chicken

Chicken, squash and spinach purée

Ingredients

- 2 tsp sunflower oil
- 50g (2oz) onion, peeled and diced
- 100g (4oz) leeks, trimmed, washed and diced
- 30g (1oz) dessert apple, peeled, cored and diced
- 50g (2oz) carrots, peeled and diced
- 150g (5oz) butternut squash, peeled and diced
- 100g (4oz) boneless, skinless chicken breast, diced
- 1 clove garlic, crushed
- 300ml (10fl oz) unsalted chicken stock
- 25g (1oz) baby spinach leaves, washed
- 15g (½oz) Parmesan, grated

When my son was a baby he refused to eat chicken until I combined it with apple. Try this tasty combination, which is a tempting introduction to chicken.

✱ Heat the oil in a saucepan. Add the onion and leeks and fry for 2 minutes. Add the apple, carrots, squash and chicken. Fry for 3 minutes, then add the garlic and fry for 1 minute. Add the stock, bring up to the boil, cover and simmer for 15 minutes. Add the spinach and cook for 1 minute. Blend until smooth using an electric hand blender. Stir in the Parmesan.

Chicken, pear, parsnip and carrot

Parsnip and pear adds a sweetness to this chicken recipe that babies love.

Ingredients
A knob of butter
1 large leek, trimmed, washed and chopped
125g (4½oz) carrots, peeled and diced
100g (4oz) pears, peeled, cored and diced
100g (4oz) parsnips, peeled and diced
100g (4oz) boneless, skinless chicken breast, chopped
300ml (10fl oz) milk

✶ Melt the butter in a saucepan. Add the leek and fry for 5 minutes until soft, then add the remaining ingredients. Bring up to the boil, cover with a lid and simmer for 15 minutes until everything is soft and cooked through. Blend until smooth or for older babies blend half, finely chop the rest and stir together.

Suitable for freezing
Suitable from 6 months
Makes 5 portions

Tomato, sweet pepper and chicken

Try this mild fruity chicken on its own, or mixed with couscous or rice if your baby can manage coarser textures.

Ingredients
60g (2½oz) onion, peeled and diced
100g (4oz) boneless, skinless chicken breast, diced
30g (1oz) red pepper, deseeded and diced
100g (4oz) carrots, peeled and diced
200g (7oz) courgettes, diced
15g (½oz) sultanas
¼ tsp mild curry powder
½ x 400g can chopped tomatoes
300ml (10fl oz) unsalted chicken stock

✶ Put all the ingredients into a saucepan, bring up to the boil, cover with a lid and simmer for 15 minutes until the vegetables are tender and the chicken is cooked through. Blend everything together until smooth.

Suitable for freezing
Suitable from 6 months
Makes 4 portions

Suitable for freezing
Suitable from 6 months
Makes 5 portions

Chicken, apricot and butternut squash

Chicken combines very well with fruit and here I've added dried apricots and apple as well as garam masala for added flavour – an aromatic mixture of ground spices used in many Indian dishes.

✶ Heat the oil in a saucepan and add the onion, apple, carrots, squash, garlic and apricots and cook, stirring, for 2 minutes. Add the remaining ingredients, bring up to the boil, cover with a lid and simmer for 15 minutes. Blend until smooth. A good way to introduce texture to your baby would be to blend half of this, finely chop the remainder and then stir the two together.

Ingredients

1 tsp olive oil
50g (2oz) onion, peeled and chopped
50g (2oz) dessert apple, peeled, cored and chopped
75g (3oz) carrots, peeled and diced
200g (7oz) butternut squash, peeled and diced
1 clove garlic, crushed
4 ready-to-eat dried apricots, chopped
1 boneless, skinless chicken breast, diced
½ tsp garam masala
400g can chopped tomatoes
100ml (3½fl oz) water

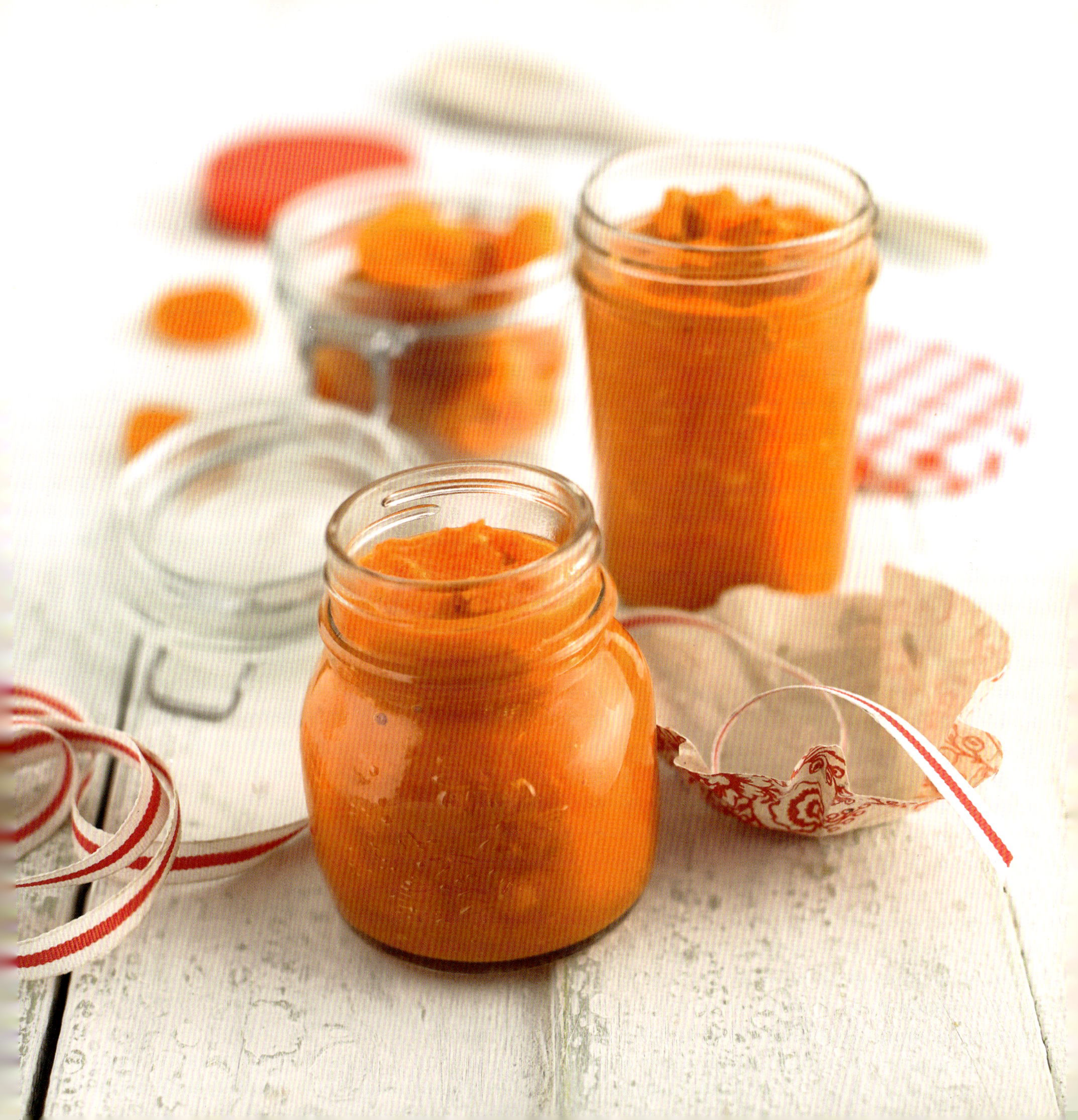

Suitable for freezing
Suitable from 6 months
Makes 4 portions

Tender beef casserole with parsnip and thyme

Ingredients

2 tsp olive oil
100g (4oz) leeks, trimmed, washed and chopped
85g (3oz) carrots, peeled and chopped
50g (2oz) parsnips, peeled and chopped
½ tsp chopped fresh thyme
85g (3oz) mushrooms, chopped
125g (4½oz) minced beef
1 tsp tomato purée
2 tsp plain flour
300ml (10fl oz) unsalted beef stock
A few drops Worcestershire sauce

It's important to introduce red meat into your baby's diet from 6 months as the iron your baby inherits starts to run out and red meat provide the best and most easily absorbed source of iron.

✻ Heat the oil in a saucepan. Add the leeks, carrots, parsnips, thyme and mushrooms and fry for 1 minute. Add the minced beef and brown with the vegetables. Add the tomato purée and flour then blend in the stock and Worcestershire sauce. Simmer for 20 minutes until tender. Blend to a chunky consistency.

Suitable for freezing
Suitable from 6 months
Makes 4 portions

Beef with lentils and tomato

A tasty and nutritious combination of minced beef, lentils, vegetables, tomatoes and cheese.

Ingredients

2 tsp olive oil
1 leek, trimmed, washed and chopped
1 courgette, chopped
1 clove garlic, crushed
20g (1oz) red lentils
100g (4oz) minced beef
400g can chopped tomatoes
20g (1oz) Parmesan, grated

✱ Heat the oil in a saucepan. Add the leek, courgette and garlic and fry for 2 minutes. Add the lentils and minced beef and fry until the meat is browned. Add the tomatoes, then cover and simmer for 20 minutes. Blitz for a few seconds using an electric hand blender or a food processor to keep the mixture chunky. Finally, stir in the Parmesan.

Suitable for freezing
Suitable from 6 months
Makes 4 portions

Beef, red pepper and carrot

A very easy recipe. The ground cumin and coriander add a lovely flavour.

Ingredients

125g (4½oz) minced beef
125g (4½oz) red onions, peeled and diced
1 clove garlic, crushed
¼ tsp ground cumin
¼ tsp ground coriander
50g (2oz) red pepper, deseeded and diced
200g (7oz) carrots, peeled and diced
400g can chopped tomatoes
100ml (3½fl oz) unsalted beef stock

✱ Put the mince and onions into a saucepan. Fry for 3 minutes, then add the remaining ingredients. Bring up to the boil, cover with a lid and simmer for 30 minutes until the vegetables are tender and the meat is cooked through. Blend until smooth or leave slightly chunky for older babies.

Tasty beef casserole

As you can't add salt to a baby's purée, I like to add herbs and spices like coriander and cumin to bring out the flavour.

Ingredients

150g (5oz) carrots, peeled and diced
50g (2oz) celery, diced
50g (2oz) onion, peeled and diced
75g (3oz) lean minced beef
30g (1oz) red pepper, deseeded and diced
100g (4oz) sweet potatoes, peeled and diced
¼ tsp ground coriander
¼ tsp ground cumin
400g can chopped tomatoes
150ml (5fl oz) weak unsalted beef stock

✱ Put all of the ingredients into a saucepan. Bring up to the boil, cover with a lid and simmer for 25 minutes until the vegetables are tender and the meat cooked through. Blend until smooth.

Suitable for freezing
Suitable from 6 months
Makes 4 portions

Beef with carrots and peas

When introducing red meat, it's good to combine it with root vegetables like carrots and parsnips.

Ingredients

2 tsp sunflower oil
1 onion, peeled and chopped
2 carrots, peeled and diced
1 parsnip, peeled and diced
125g (4½oz) minced beef
1 tsp tomato purée
200ml (7oz) unsalted beef stock
1 bay leaf
45g (2oz) frozen peas
A few drops Worcestershire sauce

✱ Heat the oil in a saucepan. Add the vegetables and fry for 2 minutes, then add the beef and brown. Stir in the tomato purée, add the stock and bay leaf, then cover and simmer for 20 minutes until tender. After 15 minutes, add the peas with the Worcestershire sauce. Remove the bay leaf then blend until smooth.

Suitable for freezing
Suitable from 6 months
Makes 3 portions

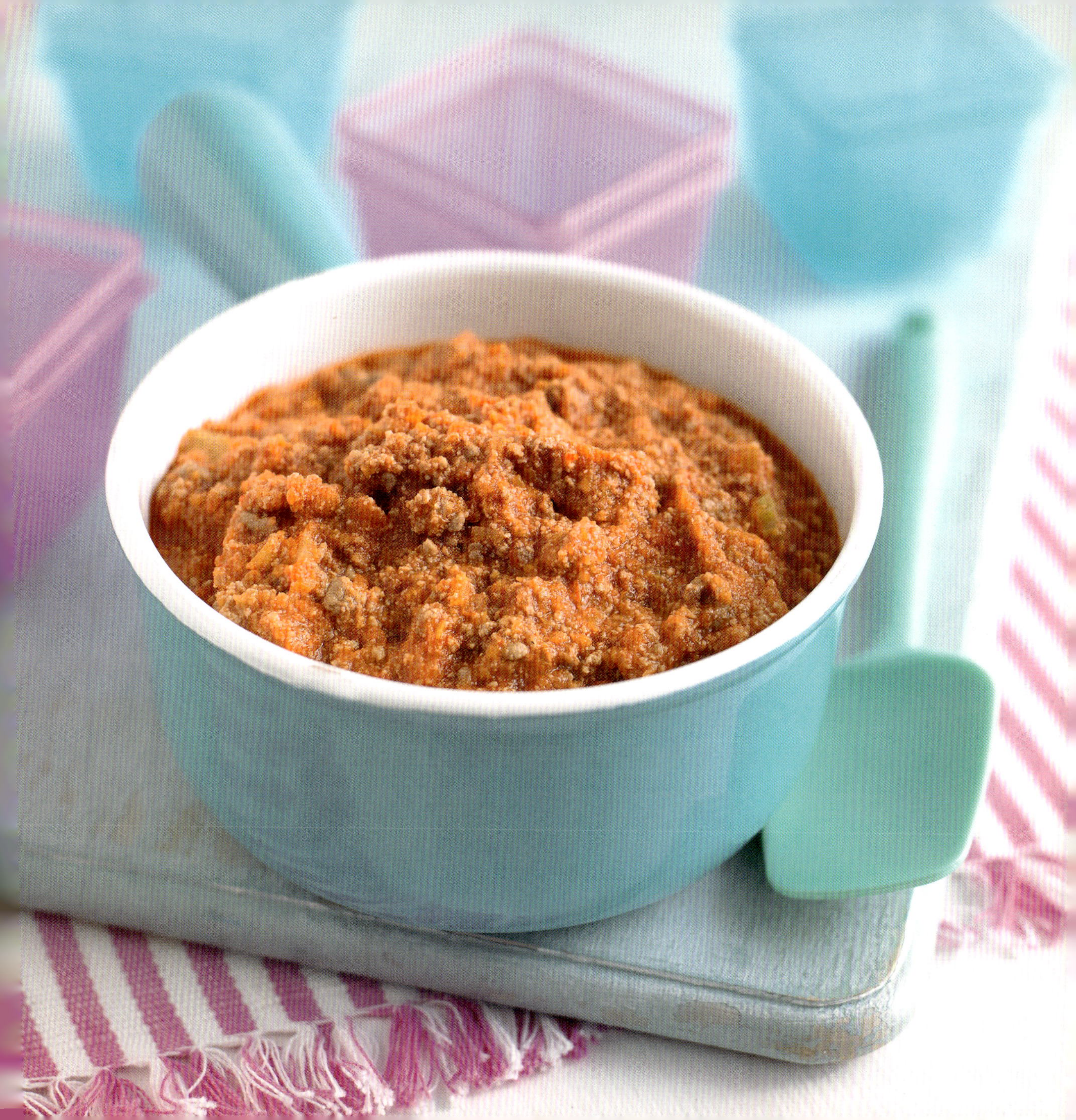

Suitable for freezing
Suitable from 6 months
Makes 5 portions

Tasty beef tagine with sweet potato

Ingredients

1 tsp sunflower oil
75g (3oz) onion, peeled and chopped
30g (1oz) red pepper, deseeded and diced
100g (4oz) courgettes, diced
100g (4oz) carrots, peeled and diced
75g (3oz) sweet potatoes, peeled and diced
100g (4oz) lean minced beef
½ tsp ground cumin
400g can chopped tomatoes
100ml (3½fl oz) water
3 tbsp pure, unsweetened apple juice

Babies are pretty open to accepting new tastes between the age of 6 and 12 months, but tend to become more fussy towards the end of the first year, so use this opportunity to introduce new flavours like this Moroccan-style tagine.

✱ Heat the oil in a saucepan. Add the vegetables and fry for 3 minutes, then add the beef and brown with the vegetables. Sprinkle in the cumin, then blend in the tomatoes, water and apple juice.

✱ Bring up to the boil, cover and simmer for 30 minutes until the vegetables are tender and the meat is cooked through. Blend until smooth.

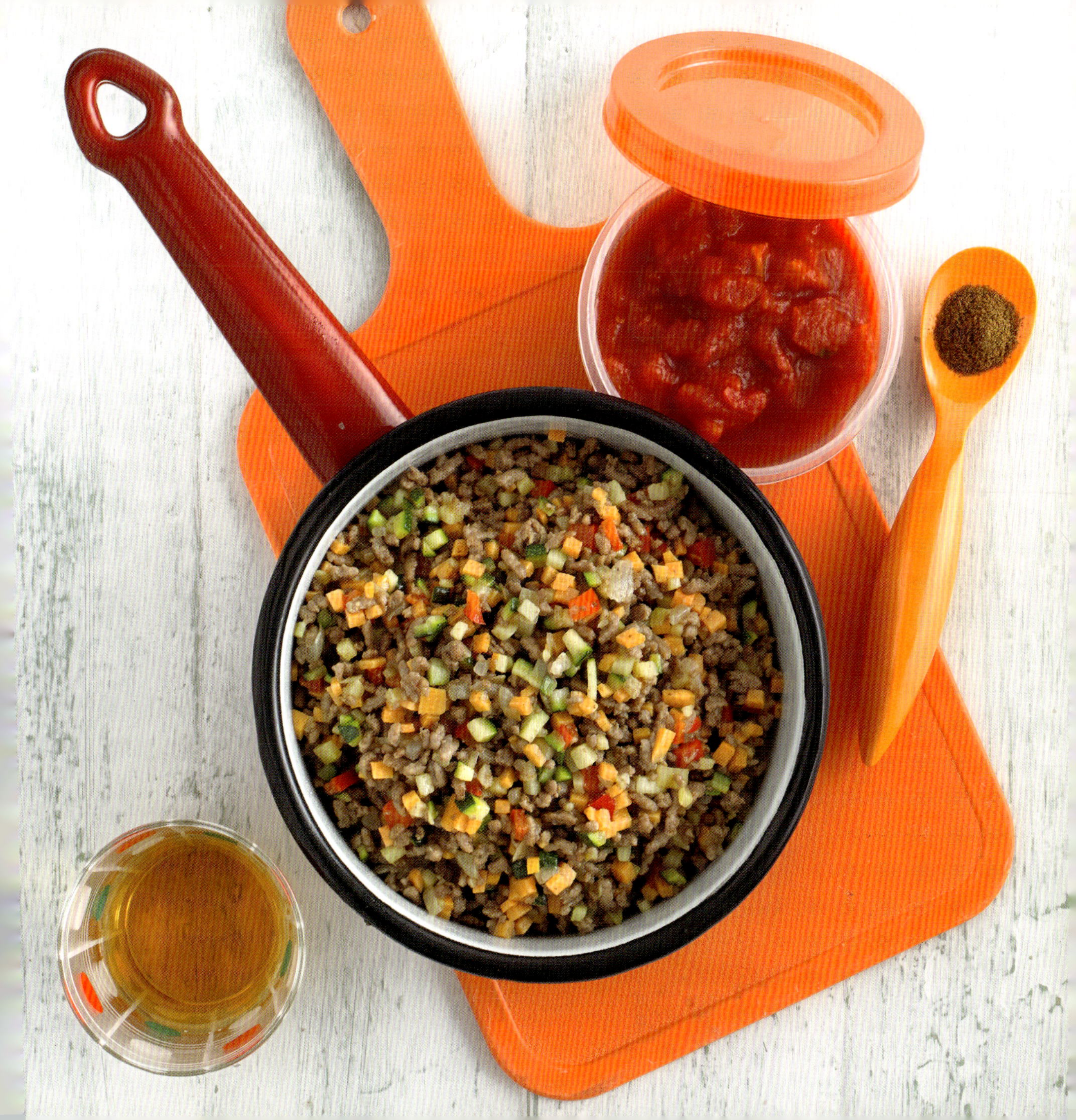

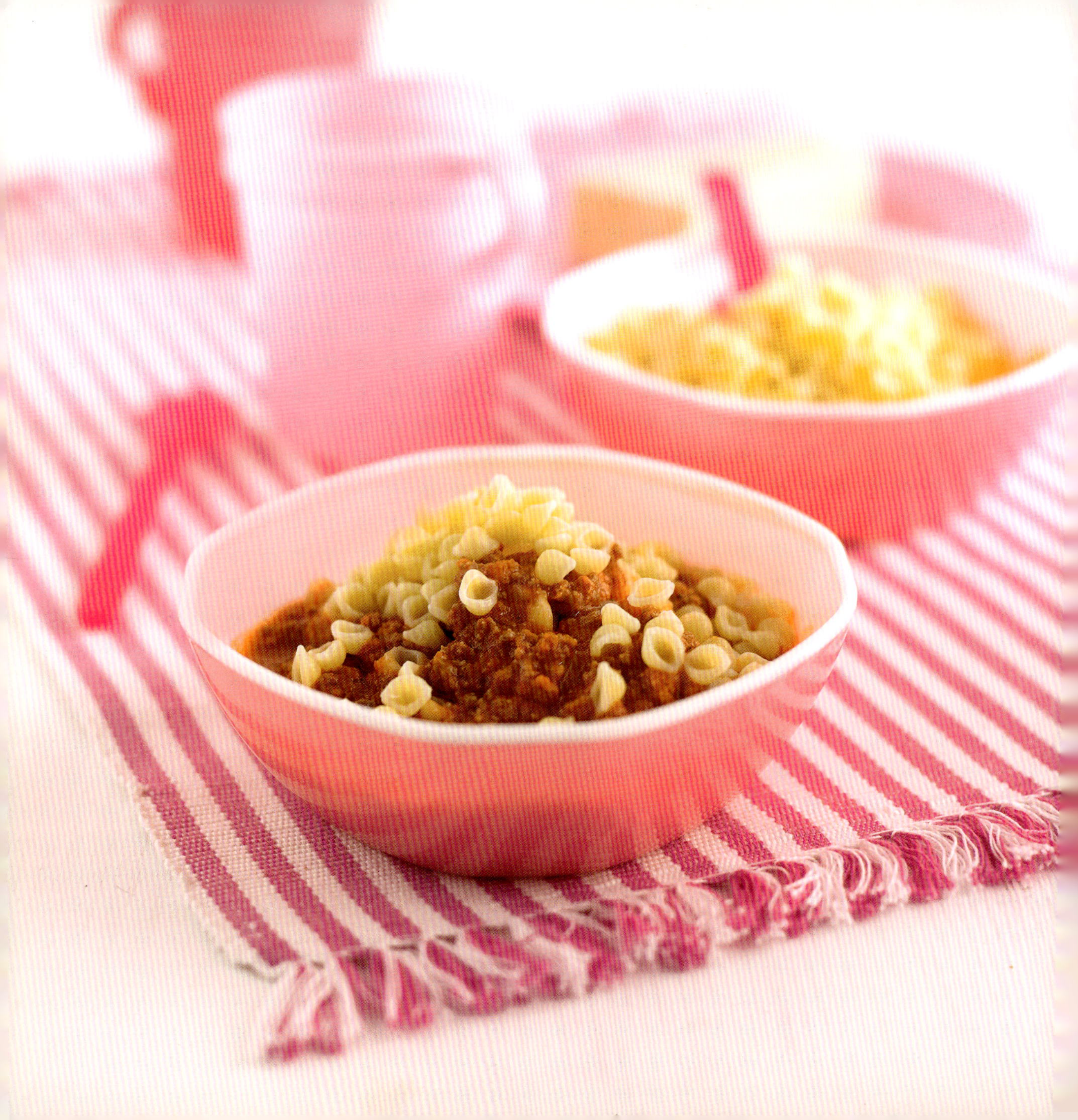

My first beef bolognese

A good way to introduce texture is to mix in small pasta shapes. Babies prefer an overall lumpy, soft texture rather than surprise lumps.

Ingredients

2 tsp olive oil
1 onion, peeled and chopped
1 stick celery, chopped
1 carrot, peeled and diced
1 clove garlic, crushed
125g (4½oz) lean minced beef
400g can chopped tomatoes
¼ tsp chopped fresh thyme
2 tbsp pure, unsweetened apple juice
2 tbsp grated Parmesan

✶ Heat the oil in a saucepan. Add the vegetables and fry for 2 minutes. Add the garlic and the beef and brown the meat. Add the tomatoes and thyme, then cover and simmer for 20 minutes until the vegetables are tender. Blend for a few seconds so that everything is very finely chopped, then stir in the apple juice and Parmesan. Serve with small cooked pasta shapes.

Suitable for freezing
Suitable from 6 months
Makes 4 portions

Beef with mushrooms and thyme

Mushrooms provide vitamin B, D, fibre and essential minerals like potassium. Adding mushrooms also helps give a smoother texture to your baby's food.

Ingredients

150g (5oz) minced beef
100g (4oz) leeks, trimmed, washed and chopped
100g (4oz) carrots, peeled and diced
200g (7oz) mushrooms, halved
1 clove garlic, crushed
4 sunblushed tomatoes
½ x 400g can chopped tomatoes
100ml (3½fl oz) unsalted beef stock
1 tsp chopped fresh thyme
15g (½oz) Parmesan, grated

✶ Put the beef, leeks, carrots, mushrooms and garlic into a saucepan and stir-fry for 2 minutes. Then add the remaining ingredients except the cheese. Bring up to the boil, cover with a lid and simmer for 30 minutes. Blend until smooth, then stir in the Parmesan until melted.

Suitable for freezing
Suitable from 6 months
Makes 4 portions

Fruit

*Suitable from 6 months
Makes 3 portions*

Blueberry, pear and banana

You can add banana to this recipe or in summer try the combination of blueberry, pear and peach. If the purée is very runny you can thicken it with some baby cereal or some crushed rusk.

Ingredients

2 ripe pears, peeled, cored and diced
150g (5oz) blueberries
1 ripe banana, peeled and sliced

✶ Put the pears and blueberries into a saucepan and simmer for 5 minutes until soft. Remove the pan from the heat, add the banana and blend the fruit until smooth.

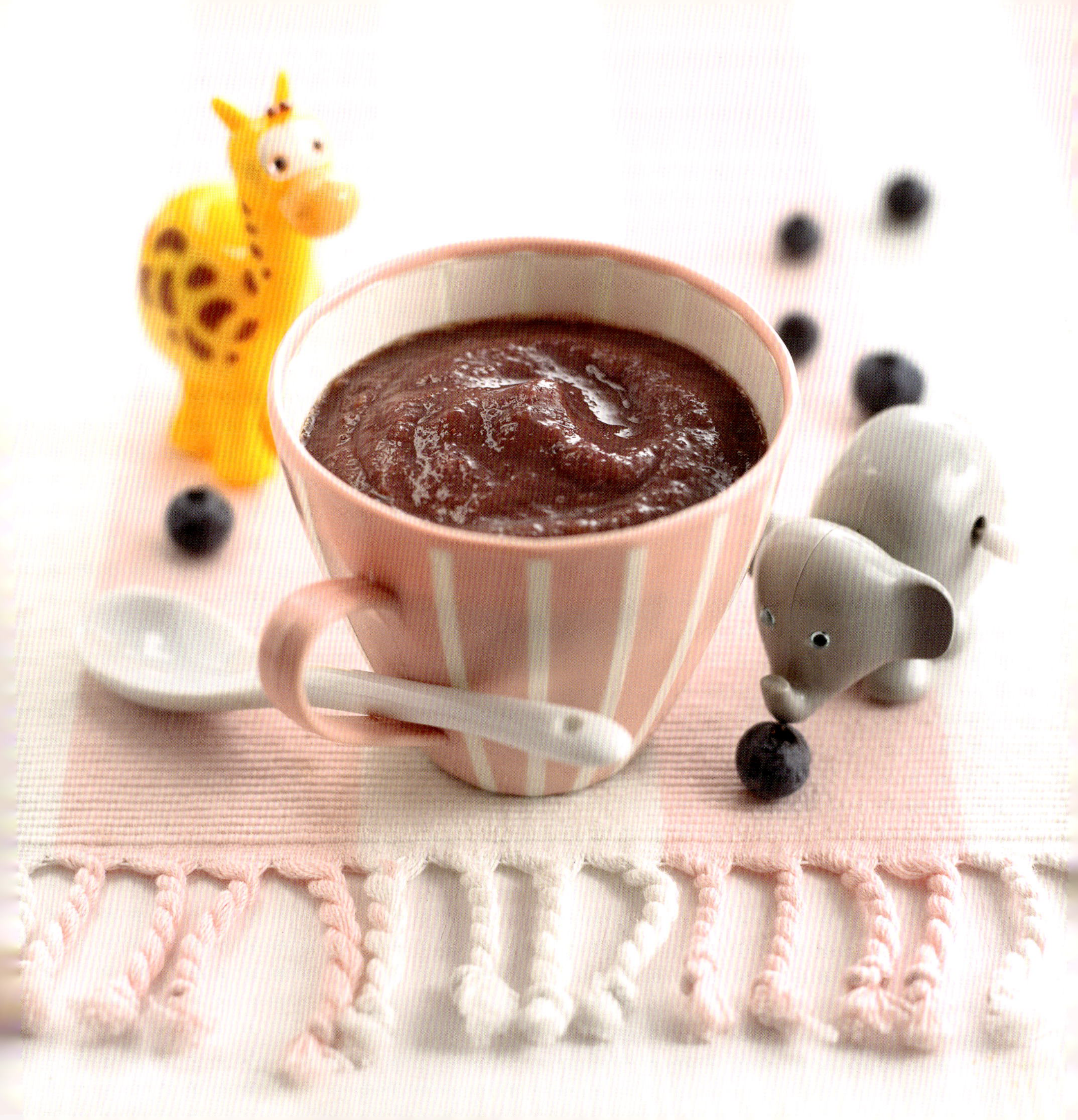

Apple and nectarine

Rich in vitamins C and A, nectarines are much like peaches. White nectarines are delicious when in season. Wash nectarines thoroughly but don't peel them as much of the goodness lies in the skin and just below.

Ingredients

2 ripe nectarines, stoned and chopped
2 dessert apples, peeled, cored and diced
30g (1oz) ready-to-eat dried apricots, chopped
50ml (2fl oz) water

✶ Put all the fruit and the water into a saucepan. Cover with a lid, then simmer for 10 minutes until soft. Blend until smooth.

*Suitable for freezing
Suitable from 6 months
Makes 3 portions*

Porridge with apple, pear and apricot

This recipe brings a fruity burst to ordinary porridge. This fruit trio works wonderfully, but you could use any fruit that is in season.

Ingredients

1 large dessert apple, peeled, cored and chopped
1 large ripe pear, peeled, cored and chopped
4 ready-to-eat dried apricots, chopped
4 tbsp water
150ml (5fl oz) milk
20g (1oz) porridge oats

✶ Put all the fruit into a saucepan with the water. Cover with a lid and simmer for about 6 minutes until tender.

✶ Meanwhile, put the milk and porridge oats into a small saucepan. Bring to the boil, then gently simmer for 3–4 minutes, stirring occasionally, until cooked.

✶ Blend the cooked fruit until smooth, then mix it into the porridge.

*Suitable for freezing
Suitable from 6 months
Makes 3 portions*

Apricot and pear purée

I don't often use fresh apricots because they can be quite sour. However recently I bought some delicious Lebanese apricots which are small, yellow and deliciously sweet.

Ingredients

250g (9oz) fresh apricots, quartered
2 ripe pears, peeled and chopped
50g (2oz) ready-to-eat dried apricots, chopped
50ml (2fl oz) water
5 tbsp natural yogurt

✱ Put all the fruit into a saucepan with the water. Cover with a lid and simmer for 10 minutes until tender. Blend until smooth. Leave to cool before mixing with the yogurt.

Suitable for freezing
Suitable from 6 months
Makes 3 portions

Porridge, apricot and banana

I used to make this for my own babies for breakfast. I used a ripe Conference pear and soft ready-to-eat dried apricots. They loved it.

Ingredients

150ml (5fl oz) milk
20g (1oz) porridge oats
8 ready-to-eat dried apricots, chopped
1 ripe pear, peeled, cored and chopped
½ ripe banana, peeled and chopped

✱ Put the milk, porridge oats and apricots into a small saucepan. Bring to the boil, then gently simmer for 3–4 minutes, stirring occasionally, until cooked. Blend with the pear and banana.

Suitable from 6 months
Makes 4 portions

9 to 12 months

Starting to feed themselves

At this stage in your baby's development, their weight gain starts to slow down. This, combined with being much more easily distracted by what is going on around them, often makes many babies less interested in food. Add in the fact that babies often prefer to start feeding themselves than be fed at this age, makes this stage frustrating at times for many parents.

Many babies also turn up their noses to anything with lumps but are happy enough to chew on finger food. From a brilliant little eater to a baby who stubbornly refuses to be fed, fussiness can start to creep in for some babies towards the end of the first year.

As hard as it is, do not pander to your baby if this happens; if they refuse food, simply take it away and let them get down to play, but do not offer them anything else. Try to hide your frustration, because if they see this they will soon learn how to get a reaction from you. Avoid letting them fill up with snacks in between meals and they will be much hungrier when the next mealtime comes round, and more willing to eat what is put in front of them.

It is important at this age to offer your baby a well-balanced diet and set the standard for the rest of their lives. You should now be aiming to include a carbohydrate, a protein, and a fruit or vegetable at every meal, and trying to meet the recommended 5-a-day for fruit and veg.

It is a good idea to let your baby try to self-feed by allowing them to use a spoon. Give your baby a small spoon or a fork with a chubby handle so that it is easy to hold and encourage them to scoop the food out of the bowl. A bowl with a strong suction base is a good idea to give them a better chance of picking up the food.

To begin with, a lot of food will end up over your baby, the chair and the floor, however, the more you allow your baby to practise this new skill, the sooner they will learn to master it. Put a clean plastic splash mat under the high chair at each meal to catch food on the floor so you can recycle it. You will need lots of patience with mealtimes as babies are far more easily distracted at this stage and would often rather play than eat.

Between 9 and 12 months is a time of growing independence, so it's important to introduce lots of finger foods and to allow your baby to start feeding himself with a spoon or fork. Remember that the more your child experiments, the quicker he will learn but you need to draw a deep breath and accept that you are going to go through a messy stage.

Milk

Continue giving breast or formula milk as your baby's main drink. Cow's milk is still not suitable as a main drink as it is low in essential vitamins and minerals like iron. However, as solid-food intake increases, milk need no longer form such a staple part of your child's diet, although they should still be drinking about 500ml of milk a day as it is an important source of protein and calcium. Many parents assume that when their baby cries it is because they want more milk, but often babies at this age are given too much milk and not enough solid food.

Your baby should now be happily drinking from a cup, with the bottle kept only for the bedtime drink of warm milk. Your baby will be teething at this age and very often sore gums can put them off eating for a while. Don't worry if your baby doesn't want to eat, they will often make up for it later that day or the next when they are feeling better. To soothe teething pains, rub a teething gel on your baby's gums or give them something very cold to chew on – this not only relieves pain but can also restore the appetite.

Foods to choose

At this stage you can be a bit more adventurous with the foods you prepare for your baby. Adding flavours using ingredients such as garlic and herbs is a great way of making food tasty while at the same time introducing them to new flavours. Children tend to be less fussy eaters if they are introduced to a variety of flavours early on in their life.

Meat and fish

Oily fish like salmon and sardines are great foods to include in your baby's diet because they contain essential fatty acids and iron, which are both important for brain and visual development. Make your own fish fingers by cutting white fish fillet into strips, coating them in flour, beaten egg and crushed cornflakes, and then frying until golden. When serving fish to your baby, check the pieces thoroughly for bones and remove any you find before you cook it.

Red meat is one of the best sources of iron. Mince is a great way to introduce red meat to babies. I find that chopping it further in a food processor once it is cooked makes it softer and easier to chew. Make a bolognese (see page 89) and mix it with tiny pasta shapes to get them used to different textures. Or make mini meatballs for a great finger food. It is best not to give processed meat such as sausages or pâté at this age.

Textures and quantities

Try to vary the consistency of the food you give; mash, grate or dice food or give whole pieces to them. Regarding quantity, at this stage your baby's appetite is still the best guide so follow this and never force your baby to eat something if they are resisting it.

Finger foods

By 9 months your baby will actively want to feed themselves and finger foods are perfect for giving them that independence and keeping your baby entertained while you prepare their meal. You can move onto more substantial finger food such as carrot or cucumber sticks, or pieces of fruit as they become more dextrous in handling food. You can also make yummy balls with chicken or salmon, or fresh fruit ice lollies – which are great for soothing sore gums.

Dried fruits

Dried fruits are a good source of fibre, iron and energy, however do not give too many of these as they can be difficult to digest and can have a laxative effect. Some dried apricots are treated with sulphur dioxide to preserve their colour; these should be avoided as they can trigger an asthma attack in susceptible babies.

Vegetables

Give soft-cooked vegetables to begin with, in pieces that are easy to hold. Gradually reduce the amount of cooking so that they are harder, making your baby chew harder. Once your baby has good coordination and improved fine motor skills, give them small vegetables such as sweetcorn or peas for them to pick up. Large pieces of raw vegetables are safer than small pieces, though, as a baby can nibble off what they can manage and it reduces the risk of choking.

Bread and rusks

Pieces of toast, rusks and pitta bread make good finger foods and can be dipped in purées and sauces. Rice cakes are also great. Many rusks on the market contain as much sugar as a sweet biscuit, so read the label or make your own (see page 170). Miniature sandwiches cut into fingers or shapes using a cookie cutter are very popular with babies, as are mini wraps.

Pasta

Pasta is a great way to introduce overall lumps and texture to your baby's meals, as well as essential carbohydrates. You can get baby pasta in all sorts of different shapes and sizes which can be served with sauces or vegetable purées. A favourite with babies is cooked pasta tossed in melted butter and sprinkled with grated cheese served with some small steamed broccoli florets.

Safety
Never leave your child unattended whilst eating, as it is very easy for a baby to choke on even very small pieces of food. Avoid giving your baby whole nuts, fruits that contain stones, whole grapes, ice cubes, olives or any other foods that could get stuck in their throat.

What to do if your baby chokes
If your baby chokes, lay them face down on your forearm or lap with their head lower than their chest. Support the head and give your baby five light slaps between their shoulders with your free hand.

Teething
Babies who are teething tend to want to bite into something cold as this soothes sore gums. You can put cucumber sticks in the fridge or banana in the freezer for a short while. You can also make fresh fruit ice lollies. Babies tend to dribble when they are teething so it's a good idea to put some Vaseline around their mouth so that it doesn't get sore.

Breakfast
Eggs are an excellent source of protein for breakfast, so you can make your baby scrambled eggs or mini omelettes that they can pick up. Just make sure that the white and yolk are cooked until solid. Cheese is important for strong bones, so sticks of cheese or fingers of grilled cheese on toast are good. You can introduce some healthy grains like wheatgerm, or mix porridge with fresh fruit compotes to boost their vitamin intake. It's important to include fresh fruit with breakfast, too, and many fruits make good finger foods.

Make mealtimes fun!
Above all, try to make mealtimes a positive experience. Have a soft toy at the chair to use as a distraction if your baby decides they are not that interested in eating, this way you can try to slip in a few mouthfuls without them really noticing. Also, try eating with your baby at the chair; babies are great mimics and seeing you eat may make them more receptive to trying food.

Many babies dislike having their faces wiped, so only wipe at the end of a meal. Use a flannel and warm water rather than baby wipes as the alcohol can sting any sore areas they may have on their chins if they are teething.

9–12 months meal planner

	Breakfast	Mid-morning	Lunch	Mid-afternoon	Tea	Bedtime
Day 1	Scrambled egg with toast Milk	Milk	Mini vegetable balls Sweet potato & apple mini muffins Water	Milk	Cod & sweetcorn fish pies Fresh fruit Water or juice	Milk
Day 2	Plum, pear & apple porridge Milk	Milk	Chicken, cheese & tomato on toast Nectarine, apple & blueberry compote Water	Milk	Mushroom pasta shells Spiced sultana rusks Apple purée Water or juice	Milk
Day 3	Weetabix with milk & chopped banana Milk	Milk	Egg mayo & tomato pinwheels Fresh fruit & yogurt dip Water	Milk	Salmon & broccoli in a cheesy sauce Spiced sultana rusks Water or juice	Milk
Day 4	Scrambled egg with cheese & tomato Milk	Milk	Savoury rice Chopped fresh fruit Water	Milk	Mini cottage pies Nectarine, apple & blueberry compote Water or juice	Milk
Day 5	Fruity Swiss muesli with yogurt & milk Milk	Milk	Tortilla pizza wedges Fruit with yogurt dip Water	Milk	Lentil & chicken curry Nectarine, apple & blueberry compote Water or juice	Milk
Day 6	Ham, tomato & cheese omelette Milk	Milk	Mini chicken sausages Pear, apple & blueberry crumble Water	Milk	Lemon sole goujons with sweet & sour sauce & sweet potato wedges Berry & yogurt ice lollies Water or juice	Milk
Day 7	Plum, pear & apple porridge Milk	Milk	Italian chicken with pasta stars Yogurt with dried fruit Water	Milk	First beef noodle stir-fry Pear, apple & blueberry crumbles Water or juice	Milk

Breakfast

Suitable from 9 months
Makes 1 portion

Scrambled egg with cheese and tomato

Ingredients

A knob of butter
½ tomato, deseeded and diced
1 egg, beaten
1 tbsp milk
1 tsp snipped chives
1 tbsp grated Parmesan

Scrambled eggs is an undisputed favourite with little ones, but adding cheese gives it more flavour and the essential fat and protein that babies need to grow.

✶ Melt the butter in a small non-stick pan. Add the tomato and fry for 30 seconds. Combine the egg and milk and pour into the pan, stirring over the heat until the eggs scramble. Add the chives and Parmesan, then immediately remove from the heat and stir until the Parmesan is melted. Serve straight away.

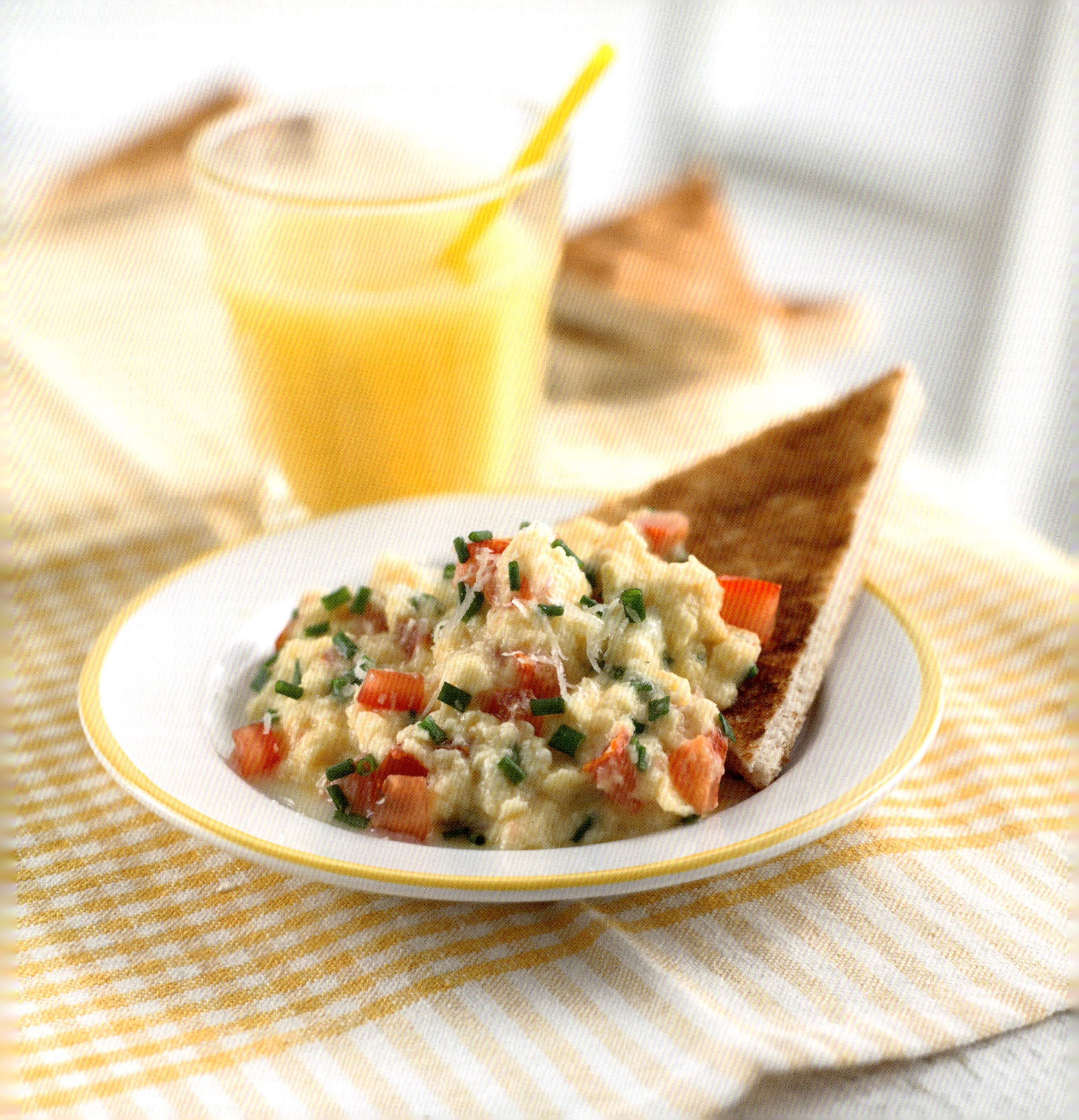

Suitable from 9 months
Makes 2-3 portions

Porridge with fruit compote

Ingredients

150g (5oz) blueberries
250g (9oz) raspberries
1½–2 tbsp caster sugar
35g (1½oz) porridge oats
250ml (9fl oz) milk

Berry fruits such as blueberries and raspberries are bursting with nutrients to give your baby's immune system a boost. Frozen fruit is a convenient alternative to fresh and is just as healthy too.

✶ Put 100g (4oz) of the blueberries and 150g (5oz) of the raspberries into a saucepan with the sugar. Stir until dissolved then simmer for 3–4 minutes until the fruits have softened. Push the fruits through a sieve into a bowl to remove the seeds and skin. Add the remaining whole fruits to the purée.

✶ Measure the porridge oats and milk into a saucepan. Bring up to the boil and simmer for 3–4 minutes until the oats are cooked. Serve with the fruit compote.

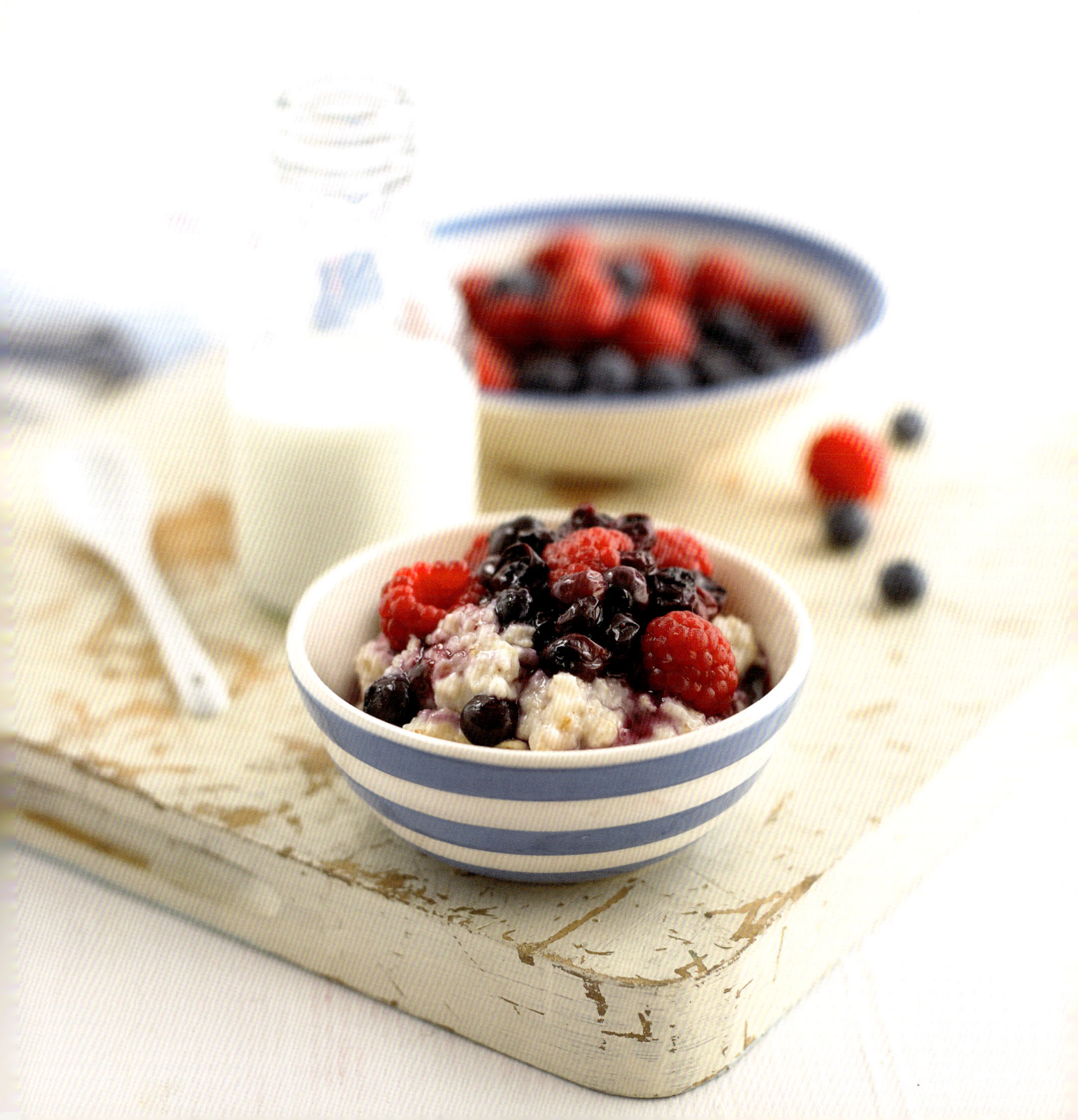

Suitable from 9 months
Makes 1 portion

Ham, tomato and cheese omelette

Ingredients
A knob of butter
1 egg
1 tbsp milk
1 tbsp grated Parmesan
½ tomato, deseeded and diced
1 slice ham, chopped

Eggs pack a powerful punch for breakfast; this protein-fuelled omelette will give your baby all the energy they need for growing up big and strong.

✶ Melt the butter in a small frying pan. Beat the egg, milk and cheese together, pour into the pan and swirl to cover the base. Cook for 30 seconds until the egg is starting to set. Sprinkle over the tomato and ham and flip over one side of the omelette to cover the ham and tomato. Continue to cook until the underside of the omelette is lightly golden and the egg is cooked through.

Vegetables

Courgette, leek and sweet potato

Suitable from 9 months
Makes 5 portions

When you think of vegetables to use for making baby food, you may not immediately think of courgettes or leeks, but they are extremely versatile and contain lots of essential vitamins. Although they are delicious and delicate in taste, their watery texture makes them better for partnering with other flavours your baby is already enjoying.

✱ Heat the oil in a saucepan. Add the leeks, courgette and potato and fry for 2 minutes. Add the thyme and tomatoes, then the stock. Simmer for 15 minutes until the vegetables are cooked. Drain the vegetables, reserving the liquid, then blend them to a chunky consistency. Add a little of the reserved cooking liquid if the purée is too thick. Stir in the cheese.

Ingredients

2 tsp olive oil
150g (5oz) leeks, trimmed, washed and chopped
200g (7oz) courgette, diced
225g (8oz) sweet potato, peeled and diced
¼ tsp chopped fresh thyme
2 tomatoes, quartered
200ml (7fl oz) unsalted vegetable stock
40g (1½oz) strong Cheddar cheese, grated

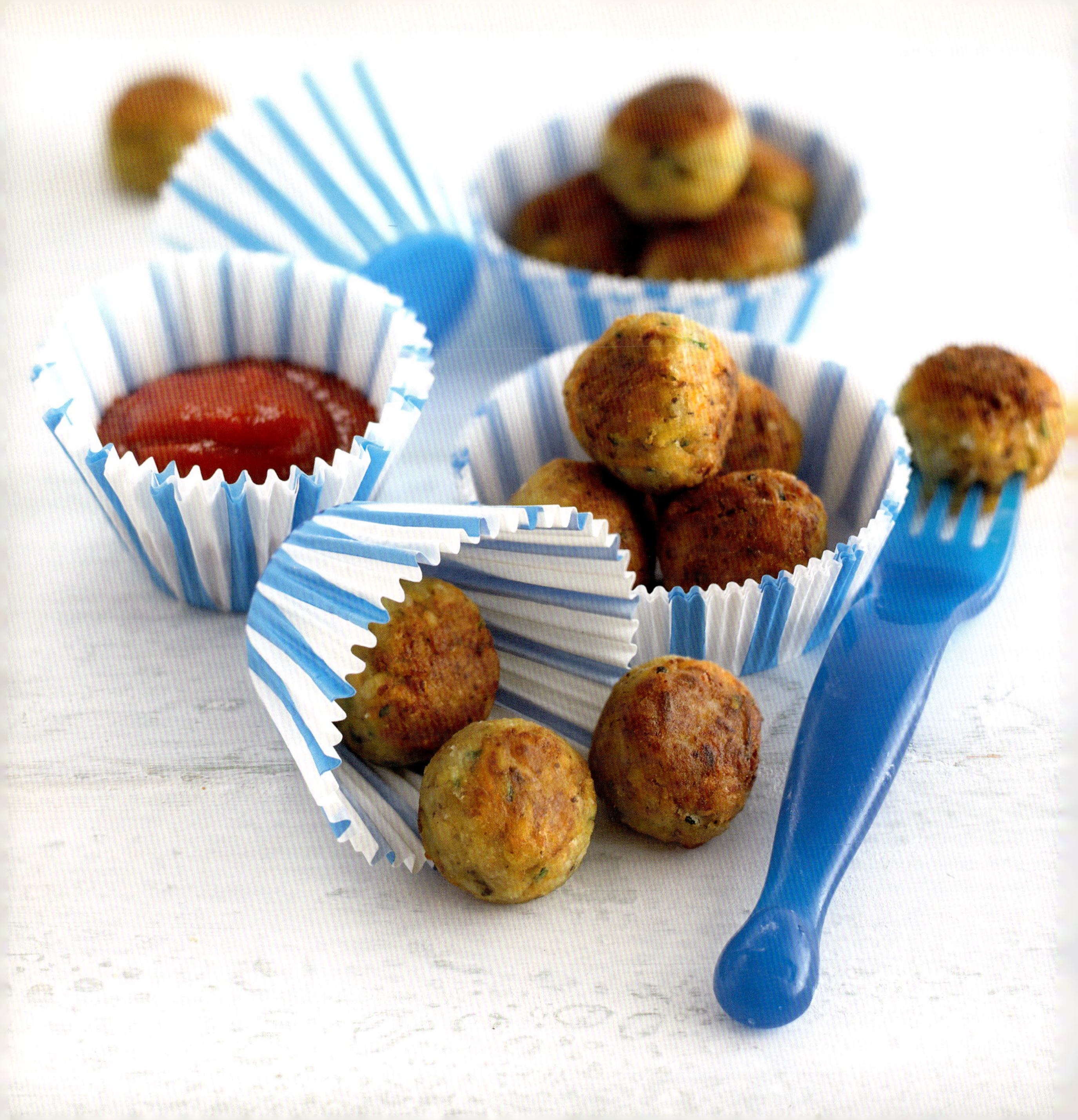

Mini vegetable balls

Suitable for freezing
Suitable from 9 months
Makes 24 veggie balls

My children loved grazing on these mini vegetable balls as babies. Full of natural flavour, this is a fantastic way to pack in a variety of nutritious vegetables, and they make an ideal finger food. If you want to freeze some for another day, freeze them on an open tray and transfer to a plastic freezer box, separating layers with greaseproof paper. Simply reheat in a microwave.

★ Put the grated carrots, courgette and squash into a clean tea towel or muslin cloth and squeeze out as much liquid as possible.

★ Tip into a mixing bowl and add all the remaining ingredients except the flour and the olive oil. Stir to combine and, using damp hands, shape the mixture into 24 little balls. Put the flour on a plate and roll the balls in it to coat.

★ Heat the oil in a large frying pan. Add the balls and fry for about 5 minutes or until lightly browned. You may need to do this in batches depending on the size of your pan.

★ Allow to cool a little and serve with ketchup.

Ingredients

- 2 carrots, peeled and grated
- 1 small courgette, grated
- 75g (3oz) butternut squash, peeled and grated
- 1 onion, peeled and finely chopped
- ½ tbsp chopped fresh thyme
- 50g (2oz) mushrooms, chopped
- 50g (2oz) Parmesan, grated
- 150g (5oz) breadcrumbs
- 1 small egg, beaten
- 1½ tbsp tomato ketchup, plus extra to serve
- 1 tsp soy sauce
- A little plain flour
- 2 tbsp olive oil

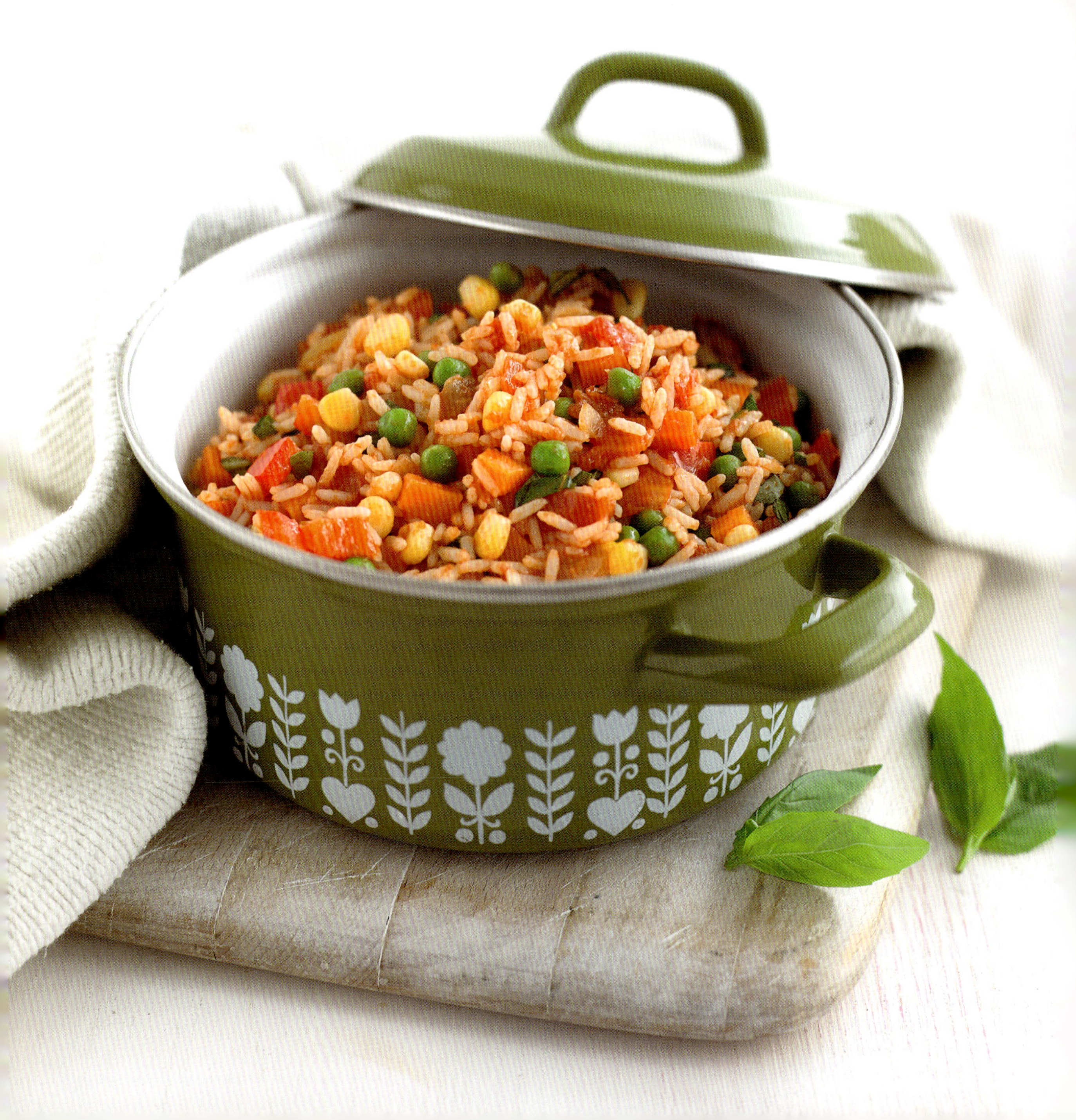

Savoury rice

Suitable from 9 months
Makes 4-6 portions

Rice dishes are good for a gradual way of introducing texture to your baby's food. You could add some diced cooked chicken to this recipe if you like.

✶ Cook the rice and carrot in a pan of boiling water for 15 minutes, adding the peas 4 minutes before the end of the cooking time. Drain.

✶ Meanwhile, heat the oil in the saucepan and fry the onion, garlic and pepper for 4-5 minutes. Add the tomatoes and sundried tomato paste and simmer for 10 minutes. Then add the rice and vegetables, sweetcorn and basil to the tomato sauce, mix everything together before serving.

Ingredients

150g (5oz) long grain rice
1 carrot, peeled and diced
50g (2oz) frozen peas
1 tbsp olive oil
1 small onion, peeled and chopped
1 clove garlic, crushed
½ red pepper, deseeded and diced
400g can chopped tomatoes
1 tbsp sundried tomato paste
4 tbsp sweetcorn, frozen or tinned
1 tbsp chopped fresh basil

Sauce suitable for freezing
Suitable from 9 months
Makes 5 portions

Tomato and vegetable pasta sauce

Ingredients

60g (2½oz) dried baby pasta
1 tbsp olive oil
½ onion, peeled and chopped
1 clove garlic, crushed
25g (1oz) carrot, grated
50g (2oz) courgette, grated
150g (5oz) tomato passata
2 tbsp pure, unsweetened apple juice
2 tsp chopped fresh basil
1 tbsp grated Parmesan

The secret ingredient to this pasta sauce is apple juice. You know how important it is for your baby to be eating a variety of veggies, and popping in a few tablespoons of apple juice will give it a natural sweetness they love. This is great made in batches and frozen.

✶ Cook the pasta in a pan of boiling water according to the packet instructions. Drain.

✶ Heat the oil in a saucepan then add the onion, garlic, carrot and courgette and fry for 3 minutes. Add the passata and apple juice and simmer for 5 minutes. Tip the pasta into the sauce with the basil and cheese.

Mushroom pasta shells

Suitable from 9 months
Makes 4 portions

Babies can now eat mushrooms. Properly cooked, they are of great nutritional value to your baby and will add a unique taste to a meal. Some babies dislike their texture, so I find chopping them finely and combining them with a deliciously creamy sauce helps. You could add some diced cooked chicken to this pasta dish.

★ Cook the pasta in a pan of boiling water according to the packet instructions. Drain.

★ Meanwhile, heat the oil in a pan, add the onion and fry it for 6–8 minutes until soft and starting to brown. Add the mushrooms and fry for 3 minutes, then add the garlic and cook for 30 seconds. Pour in the stock, then tip in the drained pasta and stir everything together over the heat. Spoon in the cream, chives and cheese and stir until the pasta is coated, then add the lemon juice to taste.

Ingredients

100g (4oz) small pasta shapes
2 tsp olive oil
1 small onion, peeled and chopped
100g (4oz) brown mushrooms, finely chopped
1 clove garlic, crushed
150ml (5fl oz) weak unsalted chicken stock
2 tbsp double cream
1 tbsp snipped fresh chives
25g (1oz) Parmesan, grated
Dash of lemon juice

Suitable from 10 months
Makes 1-2 portions

Baby pasta salad

Ingredients
50g (2oz) baby shell pasta
1 small carrot, peeled and sliced
60g (2½oz) tiny broccoli florets
50g (2oz) Emmenthal cheese, cut into cubes

Dressing
1 tbsp olive oil
2 tsp rice wine vinegar
Pinch of sugar

Salads needn't be bland. This one is really easy to make and full of goodness for your little one. Cooked broccoli florets make for great finger foods, but they taste even better when combined with other delicious flavours. Pasta is a popular option, but why not whip up a soup too?

✶ Cook the pasta and carrot in a pan of boiling water according to the pasta cooking instructions. Add the broccoli 3 minutes before the end of the cooking time. Drain and refresh in cold water.

✶ Mix all of the dressing ingredients together and add to the pasta along with the cheese. Mix well.

Carrot, tomato and cheese pasta

Suitable from 9 months
Makes 2 portions

Simple and versatile, this is one of those recipes you will use time and time again. Both carrots and tomatoes are better if cooked in a little butter or oil, as your baby absorbs the lycopene much easier. You could also include peas, mushroom or chicken.

✶ Steam the carrots for about 15 minutes or until tender. Cook the pasta in a large pan of boiling water according to the packet instructions. Drain.

✶ Melt the butter in a saucepan, add the steamed carrots and tomato and fry for 1 minute. Remove from the heat and add the cream cheese and Cheddar. Blend until smooth.

✶ Add the cooked pasta to the sauce and stir well to coat.

Ingredients

50g (2oz) carrots, peeled and diced
75g (3oz) baby pasta shells
A knob of butter
1 tomato, deseeded and diced
1 tbsp cream cheese
1 tbsp Cheddar cheese, grated

Suitable from 9 months
Makes 2 portions

Creamy carrot and tomato pasta

Ingredients

60g (2½oz) baby shell pasta
2 tsp olive oil
½ onion, peeled and chopped
50g (2oz) carrot, peeled and grated
1 clove garlic, crushed
150g (5oz) tomato passata
1 tbsp crème fraîche
1 tsp chopped fresh basil

Use full-fat crème fraîche to make a really creamy sauce. Babies still need a proportionately higher percentage of fat in their diet than adults, so avoid using low-fat variations of milk and cheese products.

✶ Cook the pasta in a pan of boiling water according to the packet instructions. Drain.

✶ Heat the oil in a saucepan, add the onion, carrot and garlic and fry for 3 minutes. Add the tomato passata and simmer for 5 minutes until the vegetables are tender. Add the crème fraîche and basil, then blend until smooth. Add the drained pasta to the sauce and stir in.

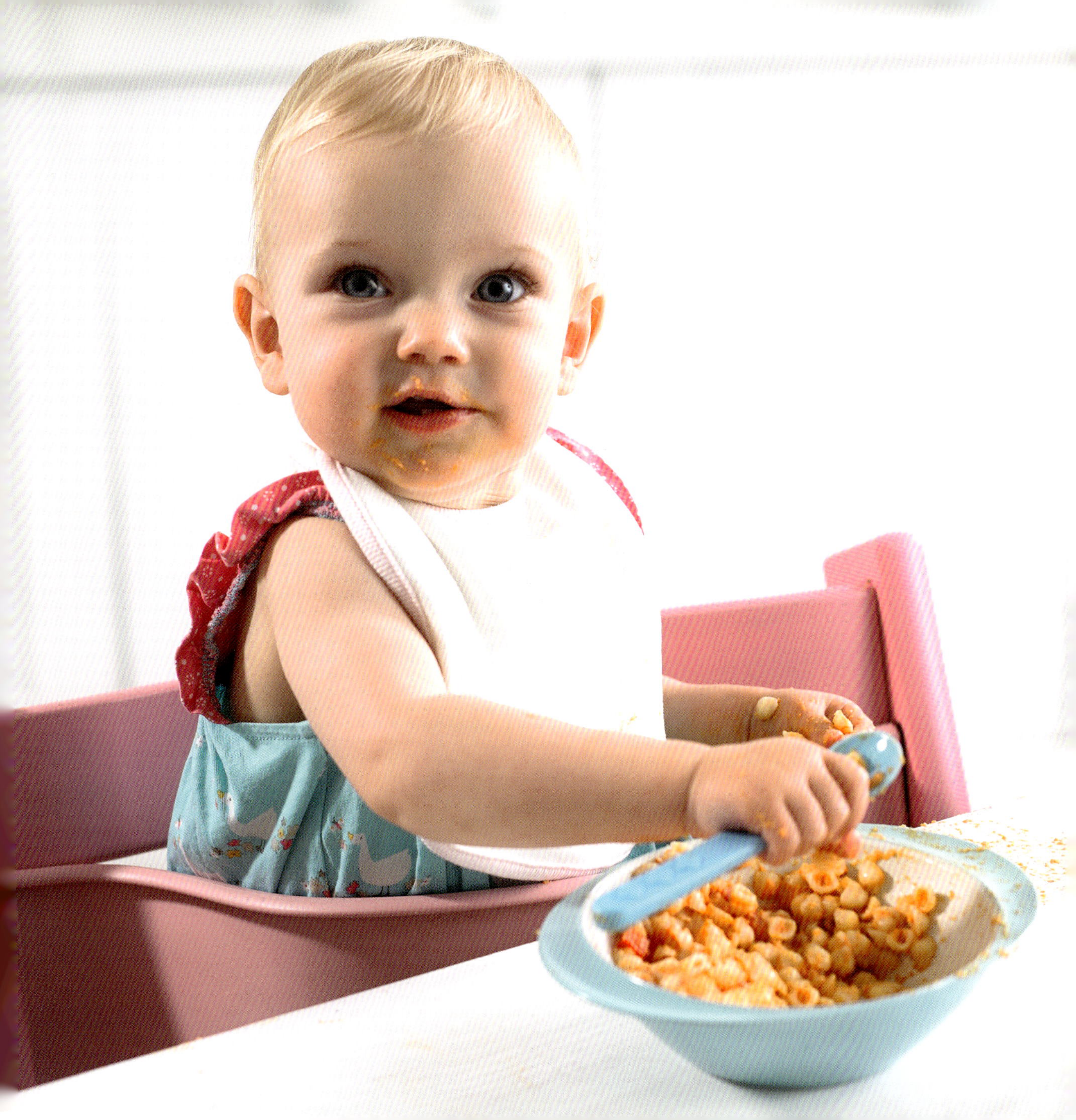

Suitable from 9 months
Makes 4 portions

Tomato, sweet potato and aubergine

Ingredients

2 tsp olive oil
1 onion, peeled and chopped
180g (6oz) aubergine, chopped
100g (4oz) red pepper, deseeded and diced
150g (5oz) sweet potato, peeled and diced
½ clove garlic, crushed
Pinch of ground ginger and cinnamon
400g can chopped tomatoes
2 tbsp pure, unsweetened apple juice

Take advantage of making your own baby food and introduce everyday spices and herbs to liven up a purée. This is a wonderful way to help expand your baby's tastebuds and get them used to the tastes of family food. As well as ginger and cinnamon, try basil, rosemary and nutmeg.

✶ Heat the oil in a saucepan and fry the onion, aubergine, pepper and sweet potato for 1 minute. Stir in the garlic and spices, then add the tomatoes and apple juice and simmer for 15 minutes until the vegetables are soft. Blend to a chunky consistency.

Chicken, squash and tomato rice

Suitable from 9 months
Makes 2 portions

This recipe is guaranteed to tickle your baby's changing tastebuds; the sweetness of the tomatoes and butternut squash mixed with rice is a mighty mini-meal filled with carbohydrates and nutrients.

✱ Cook the rice in a pan of boiling water according to the packet instructions. Drain.

✱ Heat the oil in a saucepan, then fry the onion for 2 minutes. Add the garlic, chicken and squash and cook, stirring. Then add all the remaining ingredients except the cheese. Cover and simmer for 8 minutes until the squash is cooked. Just before serving, tip in the rice and cheese and toss everything together.

Ingredients

75g (3oz) basmati rice
2 tsp olive oil
½ onion, peeled and diced
½ clove garlic, crushed
½ boneless, skinless chicken breast, diced
60g (2½oz) butternut squash, peeled and finely diced
125g (4½oz) tomato passata
½ tsp chopped fresh thyme
1 tsp chopped fresh basil
½ tsp balsamic vinegar
½ tsp sundried tomato paste
20g (1oz) Parmesan, grated

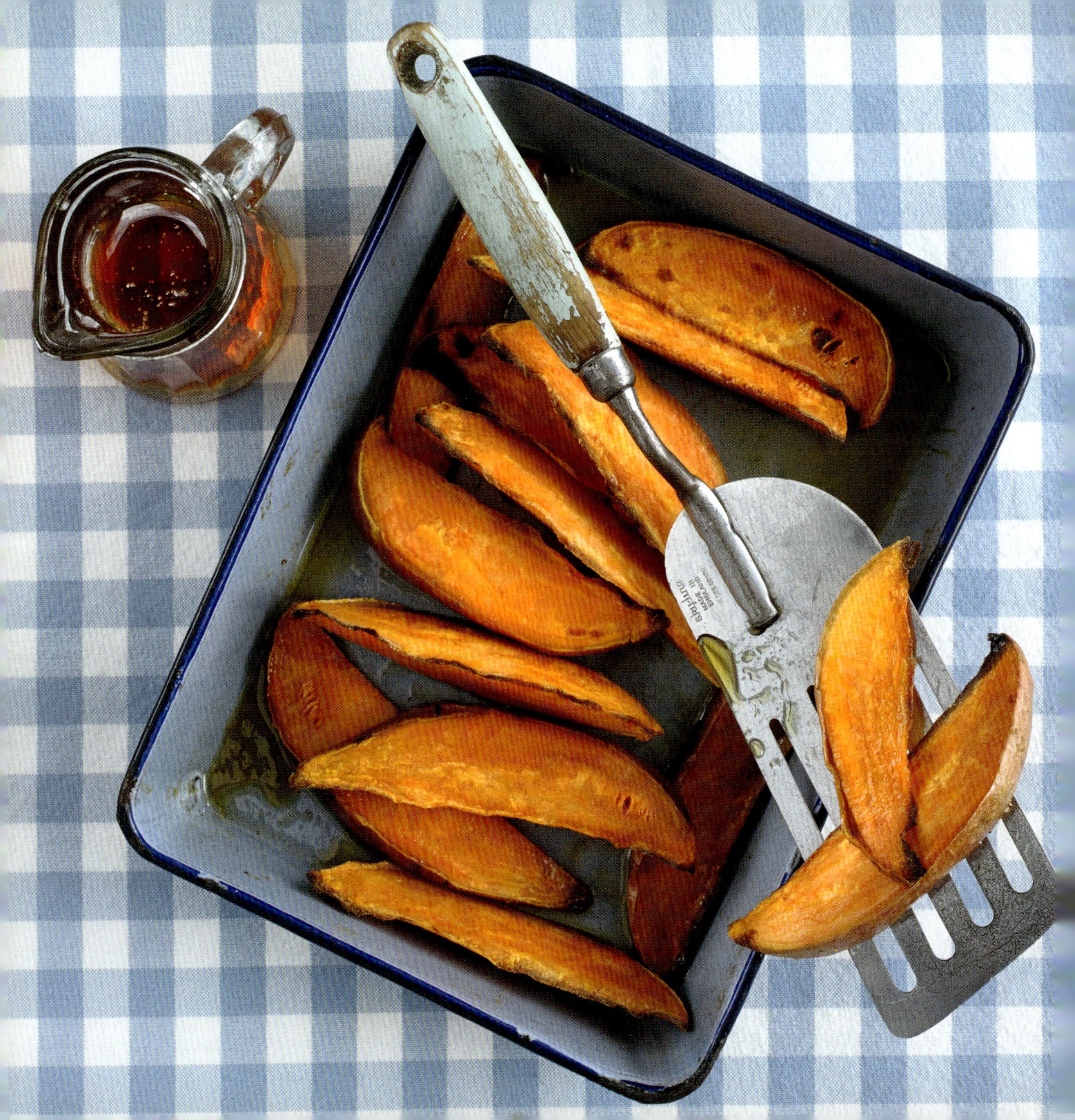

Sweet potato wedges

Suitable from 9 months
Makes about 15 wedges

This delicious finger food will have your baby grasping their pincer grip in no time. Baking sweet potatoes brings out their natural sweetness and full flavour while retaining the most nutrients. You may also peel and cube, then steam the sweet potato if you prefer.

✶ Pre-heat the oven to 200C / 400F / Gas 6.

✶ Wash and scrub the sweet potato, then slice it into wedges. Toss in the oil and arrange the wedges on a baking sheet. Scatter over the thyme, if using.

✶ Roast for 15 minutes until golden, then turn the wedges and drizzle over the maple syrup. Roast for another 3 minutes.

Ingredients
1 sweet potato
1½ tbsp olive oil
1 tsp chopped fresh thyme (optional)
1 tsp maple syrup

Suitable for freezing
Suitable from 9 months
Makes 4 portions

Chicken casserole

Ingredients

A knob of butter
1 leek, trimmed, washed and diced
50g (2oz) butternut squash, peeled and diced
50g (2oz) parsnip, peeled and diced
½ boneless, skinless chicken breast, diced
1 tbsp plain flour
250ml (9fl oz) milk
½ tsp chopped fresh thyme
25g (1oz) frozen peas
25g (1oz) Parmesan, grated

A delicious casserole for your baby, packed with veg. Serve it on its own or with mashed potato or rice.

✲ Heat the butter in a saucepan. Add the leek, squash and parsnip and fry for 3 minutes. Add the chicken then sprinkle over the flour and blend in the milk and thyme. Bring up to the boil, then cover and simmer for 10 minutes until tender. Add the peas and cook for 4 minutes. Stir in the cheese just before serving.

First chicken curry

Suitable for freezing
Suitable from 9 months
Makes 6 portions

Introducing your baby to new spices, herbs and sauces will prepare them for a lifetime of exploring new flavours. If you like you could add some baby sweetcorn to this simple curry.

✶ Heat the oil and fry the vegetables for 3 minutes. Add the ginger and curry paste, then blend in the stock, coconut milk and chutney. Bring up to the boil, then cover and simmer for 10 minutes until the vegetables are soft. Add the chicken and continue to cook for 5 minutes until it is cooked through. Serve with rice.

Ingredients

1 tsp olive oil
50g (2oz) onion, peeled and chopped
50g (2oz) yellow pepper, deseeded and diced
100g (4oz) courgette, diced
100g (4oz) butternut squash, peeled and diced
¼ tsp fresh root ginger, peeled and grated
1 tbsp mild curry paste
150ml (5fl oz) unsalted chicken stock
150ml (5fl oz) coconut milk
½ tsp mango chutney
150g (5oz) boneless, skinless chicken breast, diced

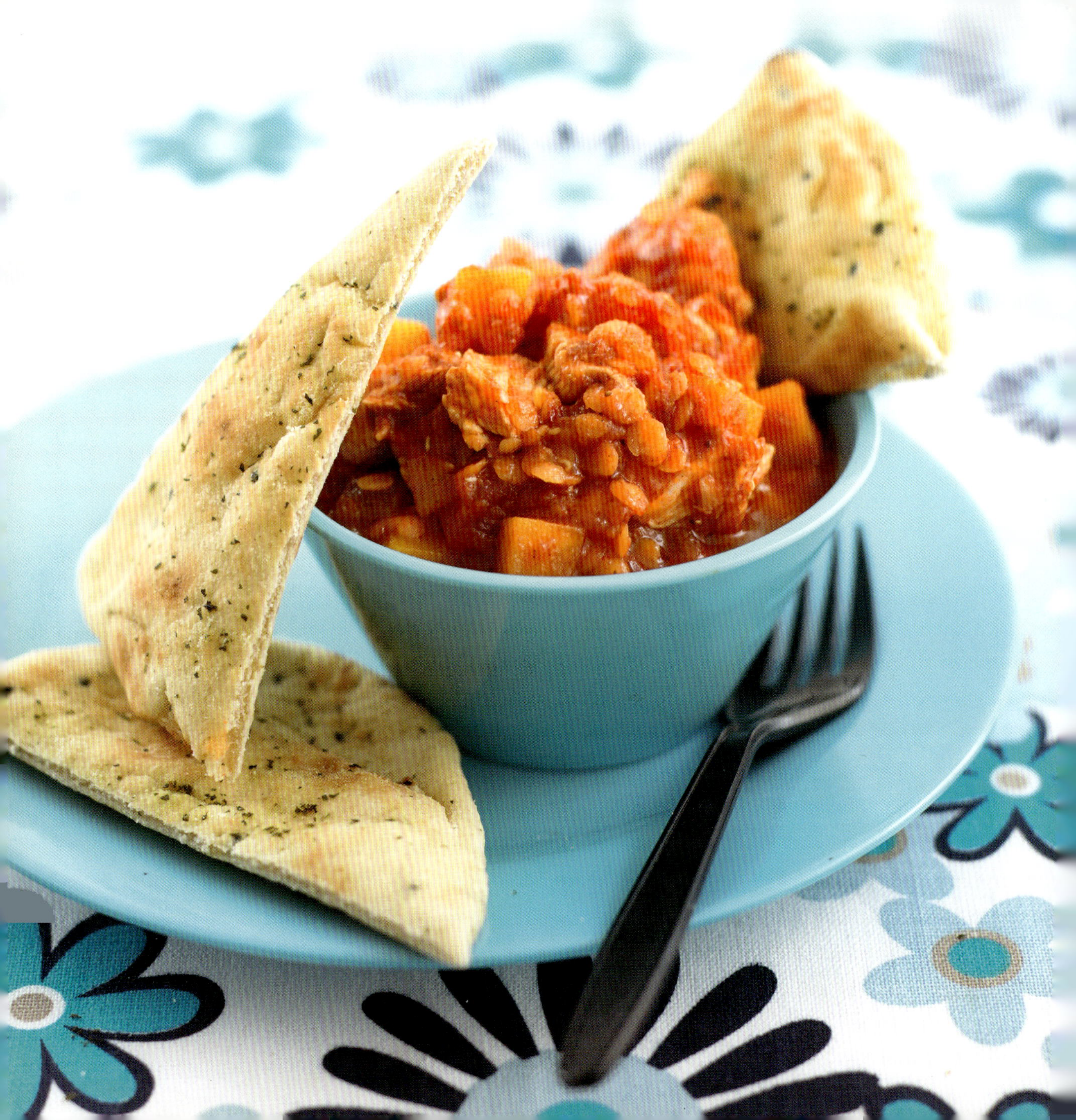

Lentil and chicken curry

Suitable for freezing
Suitable from 9 months
Makes 4-6 portions

Adding lentils to a mild curry provides a good source of protein and iron. Combined with butternut squash and tenderly cooked chicken, your baby will love this sweet flavoursome dish. For vegetarian babies, simply leave out the chicken as the pulses will provide plenty of nutrients.

* Heat the oil in a saucepan, then fry the onion and garlic for 2 minutes. Add the curry paste and lentils, then stir in the tomatoes. Cover with a lid and simmer for 10 minutes. Add the chicken stock, squash, chicken chunks and mango chutney and simmer for another 10 minutes until tender.

Ingredients

2 tsp olive oil
½ onion, peeled and diced
1 clove garlic, crushed
2 tsp mild curry paste
20g (1oz) red lentils
400g can chopped tomatoes
100ml (4fl oz) unsalted chicken stock
75g (3oz) butternut squash, peeled and diced
1 boneless, skinless chicken breast, diced
½ tsp mango chutney

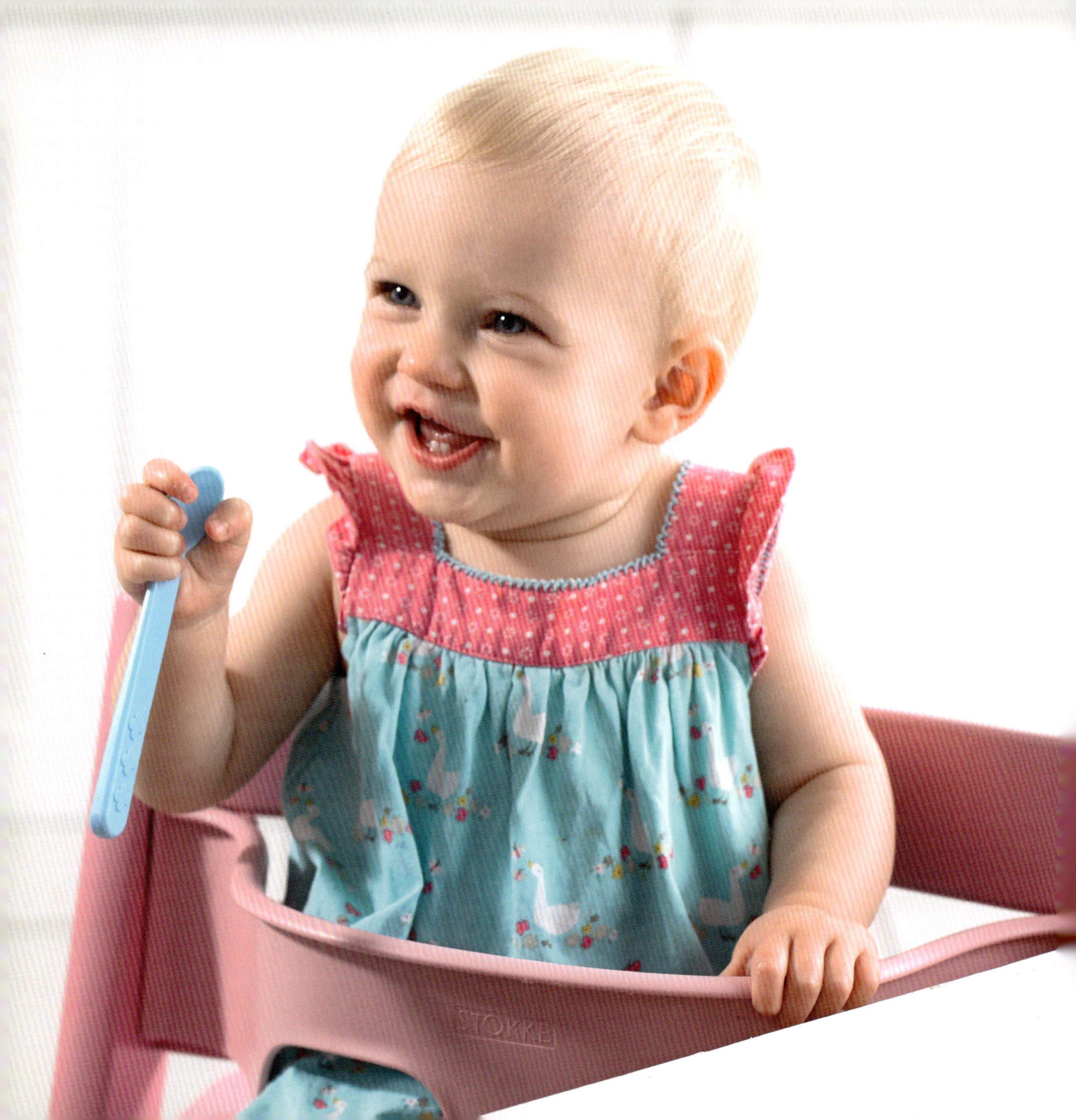
STOKKE

Italian chicken with pasta stars

Suitable for freezing
Suitable from 9 months
Makes 5 portions

You'll only need to travel as far as your fridge to find the ingredients for this Italian medley. Introduce your baby to a world of flavours early on and you'll soon have them clearing their plates at the dinner table.

✱ Cook the pasta in a pan of boiling water according to the packet instructions. Drain.

✱ Heat the oil in a saucepan and fry the leek and pepper for 3 minutes. Add the garlic and fry for 30 seconds, then tip in the tomatoes, stock, purée and basil. Cook for 5 minutes, then add the chicken and simmer for 5–8 minutes until cooked through. Add the pasta and cheese and stir together to combine.

Ingredients

75g (3oz) pasta stars (or other tiny shapes)
1 tsp olive oil
50g (2oz) leek, trimmed, washed and chopped
50g (2oz) red pepper, deseeded and diced
1 clove garlic, crushed
½ x 400g can chopped tomatoes
150ml (5fl oz) unsalted chicken stock
1 tsp tomato purée
2 tsp chopped fresh basil
100g (4oz) boneless, skinless chicken breast, diced
20g (1oz) Parmesan, grated

Suitable from 9 months
Makes 12

Mini chicken sausages

Ingredients

75g (3oz) carrot, peeled and grated
25g (1oz) red pepper, deseeded and diced
15g (½oz) spring onions, sliced
30g (1oz) dessert apple, peeled and grated
2 tsp chopped fresh thyme
225g (8oz) minced chicken or turkey
75g (3oz) breadcrumbs
50g (2oz) Parmesan, grated
Olive oil, for drizzling

These tot-friendly chicken sausages are packed full of flavour and are a great way to sneak in those all-important vegetables. Little ones will love them too as they make the perfect finger food.

✶ Pre-heat the oven to 200C / 400F / Gas 6.

✶ Put the carrot, pepper, spring onions and apple into a food processor and whiz until finely chopped. Add all the remaining ingredients and whiz again until blended. With damp hands, shape the mixture into 12 sausages, then set aside to chill for 10 minutes.

✶ Place the sausages on a baking sheet lined with non-stick paper. Drizzle over a little oil and bake in the oven for 15 minutes, turning over halfway through the cooking time.

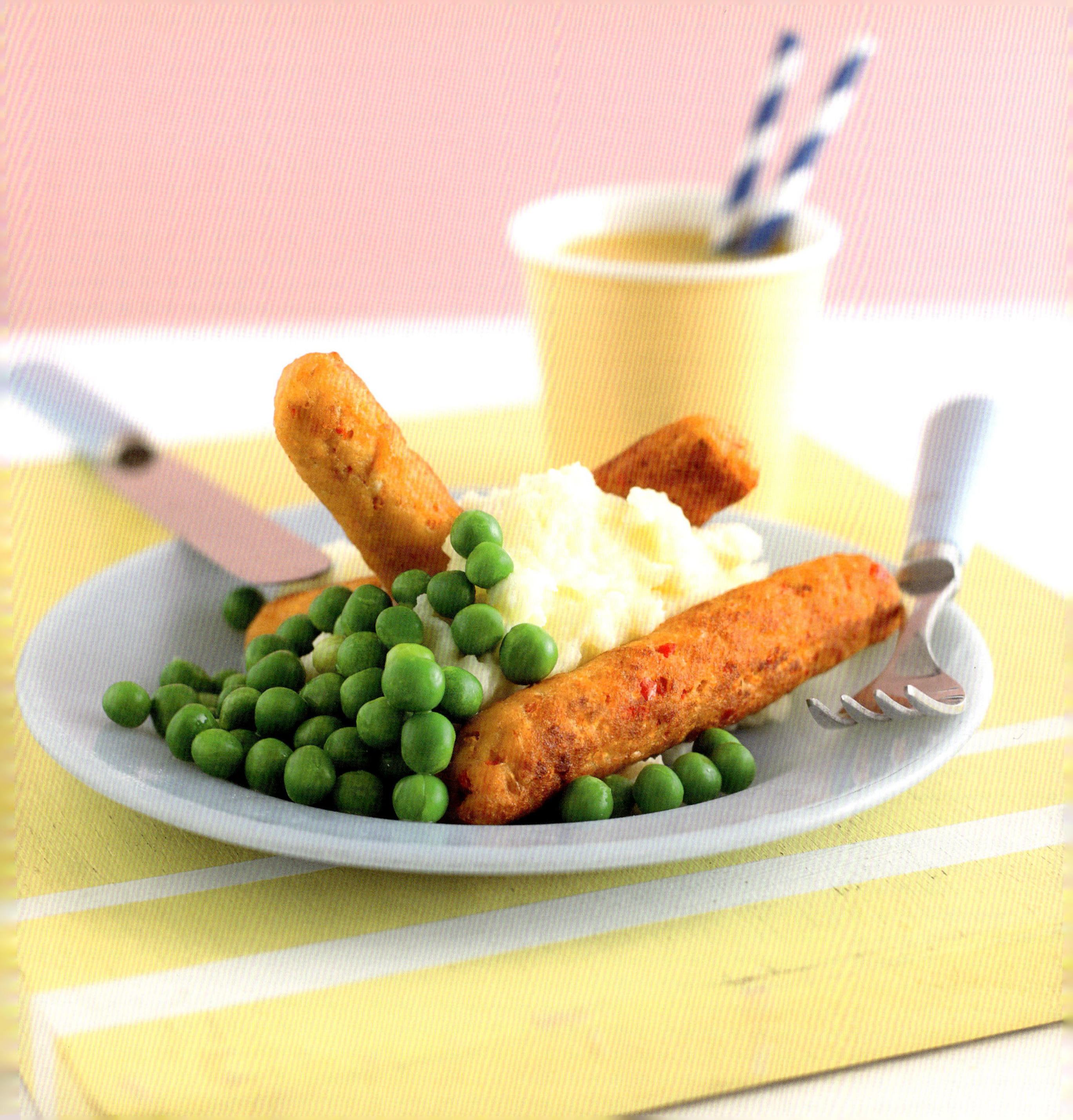

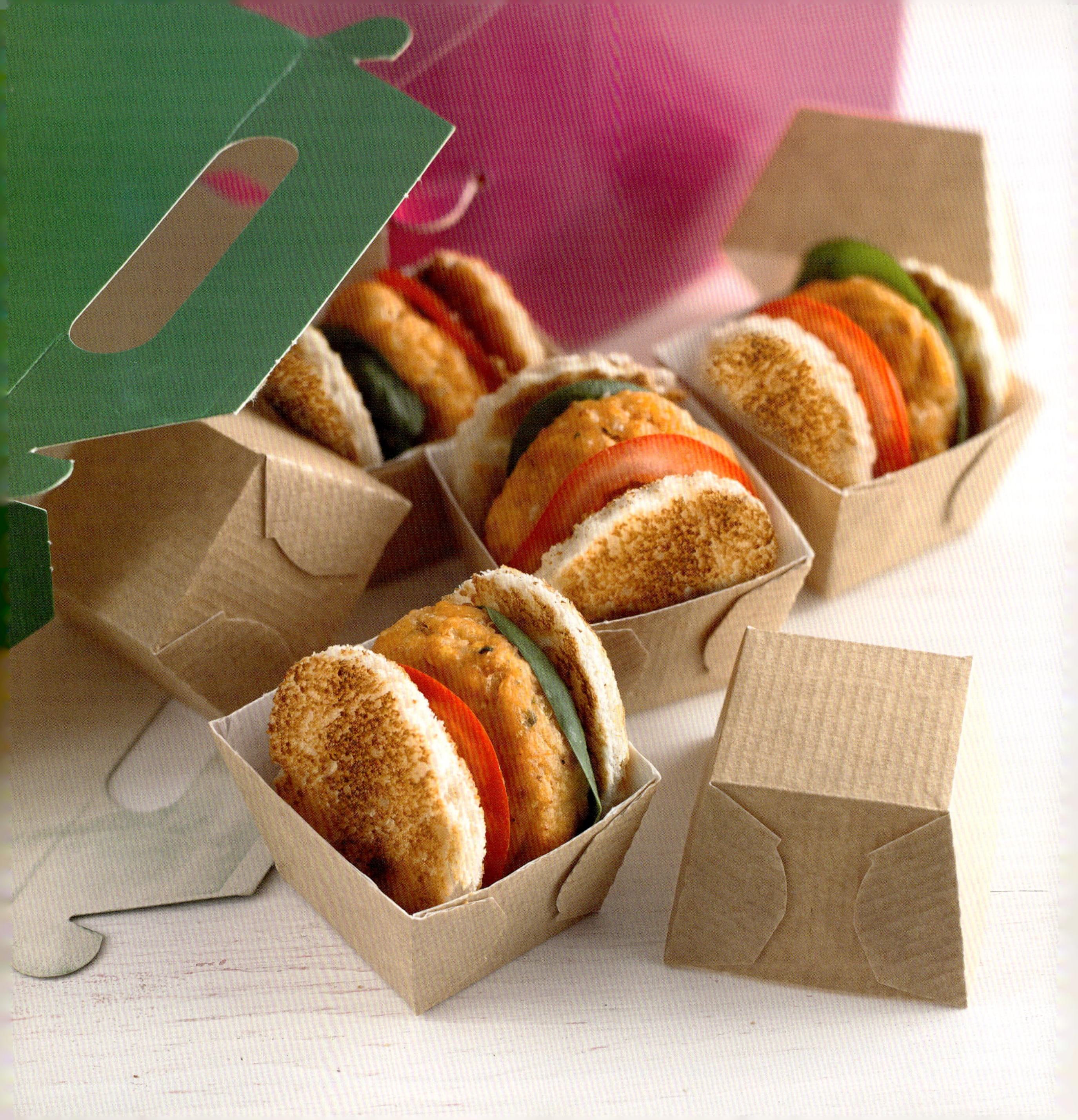

Mini turkey burgers

Suitable from 9 months
Makes 15 mini burgers

Mini turkey burgers are a fun and easy way to satisfy growing appetites – plus they can easily be made up in batches for the week ahead. A little tip; they'll go down a treat with my sweet potato wedges.

✱ Pre-heat the oven to 200C / 400F / Gas 6.

✱ Put the onion, apple and thyme into a food processor and whiz until everything is finely chopped. Add the remaining ingredients and whiz again until they are all combined. With damp hands, shape the mixture into 15 mini burgers. Place the burgers on a baking sheet lined with non-stick paper and drizzle over a little oil. Bake in the oven for 8–10 minutes, then turn over and cook for another 8–10 minutes until golden and cooked through.

Ingredients

½ onion, peeled and chopped
½ dessert apple, peeled and grated
1 tsp chopped fresh thyme
250g (9oz) minced turkey
75g (3oz) white breadcrumbs
40g (1½oz) Cheddar cheese, grated
2 tbsp tomato ketchup
A few drops Worcestershire sauce
Olive oil, for drizzling

Suitable from 12 months
Makes 8 fingers

Chicken, cheese and tomato on toast

Ingredients

2 slices wholemeal bread
A knob of butter
50g (2oz) cooked chicken, chopped
20g (1oz) Cheddar cheese, grated
1 tbsp snipped fresh chives
1 tbsp mayonnaise
1 tomato, deseeded and diced

Good old cheese on toast is a firm favourite in many households, but why not add a protein-rich twist for a more substantial meal? Chicken is an easy win with tots – especially with this recipe.

★ Pre-heat the grill.

★ Toast the bread in a toaster then butter one side and place it on a baking tray. Mix the chicken, Cheddar, chives, mayonnaise and tomato together and spread on top of the toast.

★ Grill until bubbling. Remove the crusts, then slice each toast into four strips.

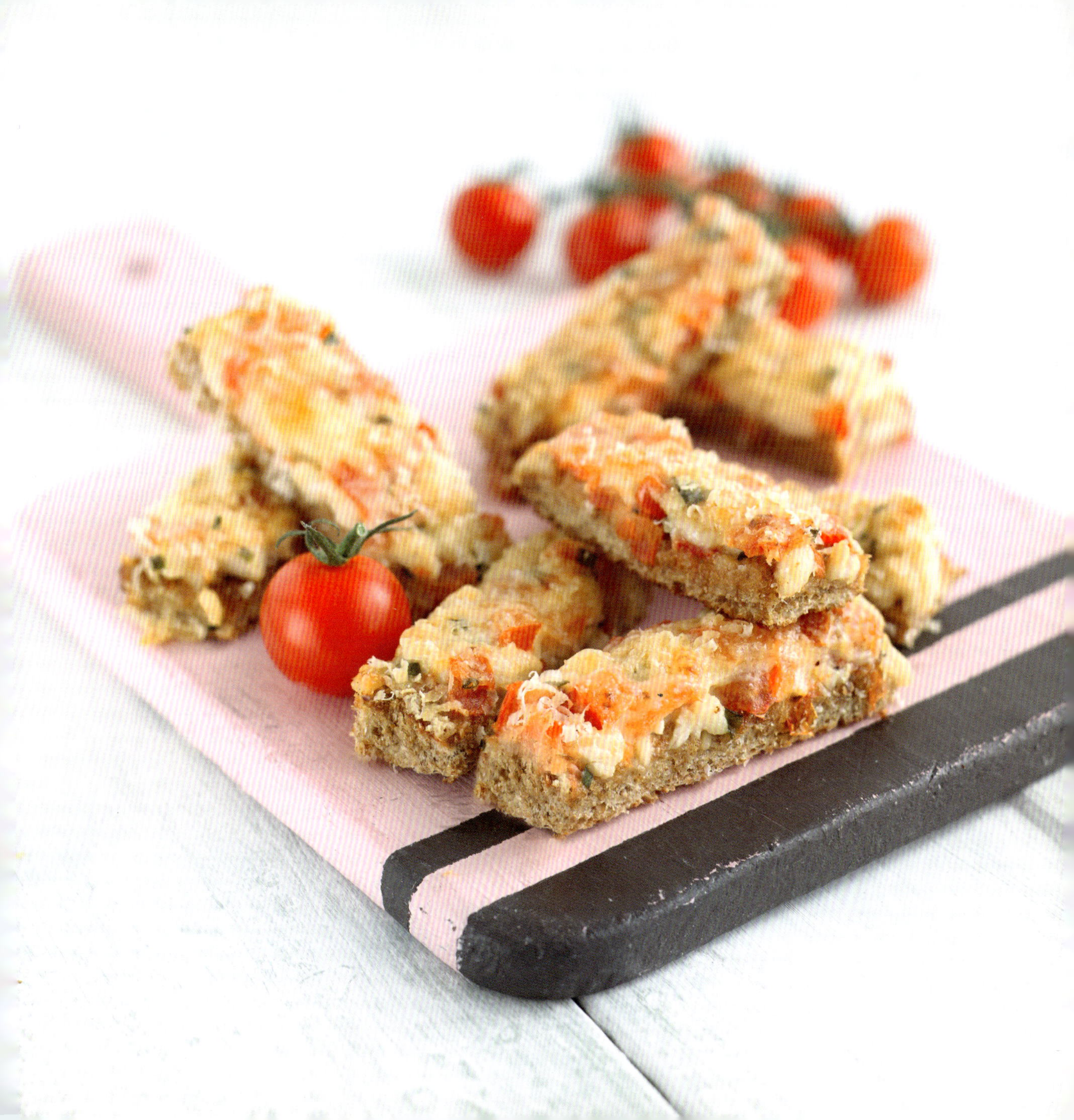

Suitable from 9 months

Makes 3-4 portions

Sweet potato mash with chicken

Ingredients

175g (6oz) sweet potatoes, peeled and diced
175g (6oz) potatoes, peeled and diced
25g (1oz) Parmesan, grated
3 tbsp milk
A knob of butter
50g (2oz) cooked chicken, diced

Chicken is high in protein and one of the most easily digested meats you'll feed to your baby. The darker meat, such as thighs and legs, is higher in iron and fat which your growing baby needs, so make sure you include a good mix. Turkey also makes a great first meat for baby.

As a variation, if you want to leave out the chicken, simply replace it with 50g (2oz) broccoli florets which have been steamed for 4 minutes. Mash them into the potatoes once cooked.

✱ Cook the potatoes in boiling salted water for 15–20 minutes until tender. Drain and mash with the Parmesan, milk and butter. Stir in the chicken pieces.

Chicken, sweetcorn and tarragon pasta

Suitable from 9 months
Makes 3-4 portions

I love to use herbs and spices to bring my recipes to life. Here, I've added a zing to this classic chicken and white sauce with a touch of tarragon. You could also experiment with coriander, garlic, oregano and sage.

✶ Cook the pasta in a pan of boiling water according to the packet instructions. Drain.

✶ Melt the butter in a saucepan. Add the flour, then blend in the milk, stirring until the sauce is smooth and thickened, then stir in the chicken, sweetcorn and tarragon. Add the drained pasta to the sauce with the cheese.

Ingredients

- 60g (2½oz) baby pasta
- 15g (½oz) butter
- 1½ tbsp plain flour
- 200ml (7fl oz) milk
- 30g (1oz) cooked chicken breast, diced
- 3 tbsp sweetcorn, frozen or canned
- ¼ tsp chopped fresh tarragon
- 50g (2oz) Parmesan, grated

Chicken, tomato and spinach pasta

Suitable from 9 months
Makes 2 portions

Ingredients

75g (3oz) baby pasta shells
2 tsp olive oil
½ onion, peeled and finely diced
½ clove garlic, crushed
125g (4½oz) tomato passata
1 tsp sundried tomato paste
15g (½oz) baby spinach leaves, washed, drained and chopped
30g (1oz) cooked chicken, diced
15g (½oz) Parmesan, grated
1 tsp chopped fresh basil

This chicken pasta recipe is a great way of getting those all-important super-veggies into their diet. Baby spinach is my favourite, but you can also try broccoli and peas.

★ Cook the pasta in a pan of boiling water according to the packet instructions. Drain.

★ Heat the oil in a saucepan. Add the onion and fry for 5 minutes, then add the garlic, passata and sundried tomato paste and simmer for 2 minutes. Add the spinach, chicken, Parmesan and basil and heat through, then toss in the pasta.

Fish

Salmon and broccoli in a cheesy sauce

Suitable from 9 months
Makes 3 portions

Fish is quick and easy to prepare and combining it with vitamin-rich vegetables such as broccoli is a tasty way to develop your baby's palate. This is also good as a sauce with little pasta shapes.

★ Melt the butter in a saucepan and fry the onion for 5 minutes until soft. Add the vinegar and stir until evaporated, then stir in the flour and blend in the milk.

★ Cook, stirring, until thickened. Carefully stir in the salmon and simmer for 3 minutes, then stir in the Parmesan and lemon juice.

★ Meanwhile, cook the broccoli florets in a pan of boiling water for 4 minutes until tender, then gently stir through the salmon and cheese sauce, trying not to break up the fish chunks.

Ingredients

25g (1oz) butter
1 onion, peeled and finely chopped
2 tsp rice wine vinegar
2 tbsp plain flour
300ml (10fl oz) milk
200g (7oz) boneless, skinless salmon fillet, chopped into 3cm (1in) cubes
25g (1oz) Parmesan, grated
1 tsp lemon juice
50g (2oz) broccoli florets

Suitable from 12 months
Make about 12 pieces

Lemon sole goujons with sweet and sour sauce

Goujons

4 boneless, skinless lemon sole fillets
50g (2oz) Panko breadcrumbs
50g (2oz) Parmesan, finely grated
Pinch of cayenne pepper
50g (2oz) plain flour
2 eggs, beaten
3 tbsp sunflower oil
A knob of butter

Sauce

1 tbsp rice wine vinegar
3 tbsp tomato ketchup
1 tbsp soy sauce
1½ tbsp caster sugar
1 tbsp cornflour

Fish contains all sorts of wonderfully healthy nutrients that your growing baby needs. I like to serve these deliciously crisp goujons with a sweet and sour sauce, but you could opt for a little tomato ketchup or tartar sauce for dipping.

✳ Slice the sole fillets into large strips (3 or 4 from each fillet). Mix the breadcrumbs, cheese and cayenne pepper together in a shallow bowl. Put the flour and beaten eggs into separate bowls then coat the fish first in the flour, then the egg, then the breadcrumbs.

✳ Heat the oil and butter in a frying pan and fry the goujons for 2 minutes each side until crispy. Drain on kitchen paper.

✳ For the sauce, measure the vinegar, ketchup, soy sauce, caster sugar and 5 tablespoons of cold water into a saucepan. Mix the cornflour into the sauce and stir until blended and smooth. Cook over a low heat, stirring, until thickened. Serve the sauce with the goujons.

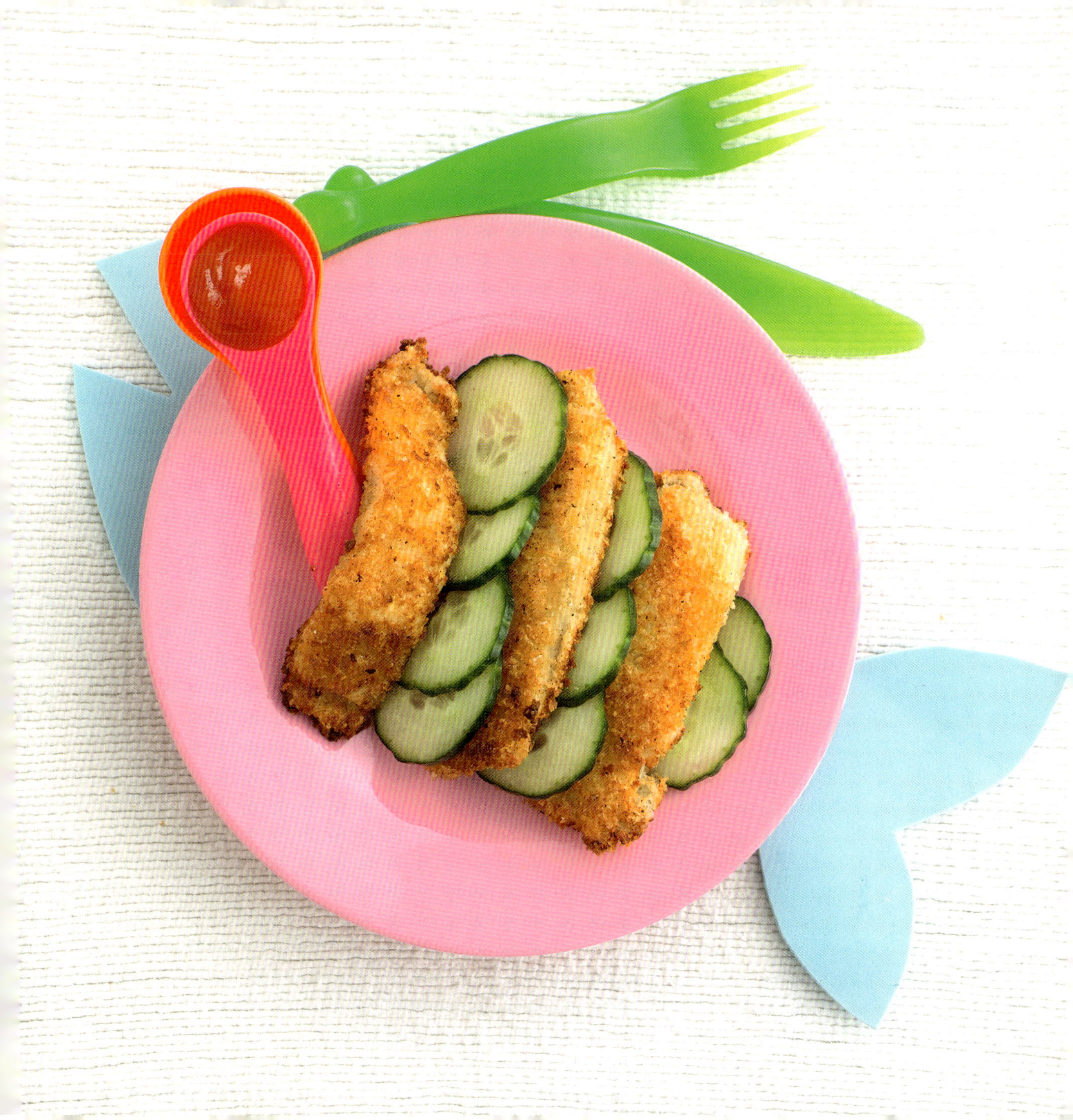

Suitable from 9 months
Makes 16 fish cakes

Tuna and sweetcorn fish cakes

Ingredients

250g (9oz) potatoes, peeled and diced
160g can of tuna, drained
35g (1½oz) white breadcrumbs
1 tbsp tomato ketchup
3 tbsp light mayonnaise
3 tbsp sweetcorn, frozen or canned
1 tbsp snipped fresh chives
25g (1oz) Parmesan, grated
A little plain flour
2 tbsp olive oil

Fish cakes are a classic for a good reason; they're easy to make and yummy to eat. I make these for a light weekend lunch or a quick and tasty midweek meal – especially if I have any potatoes that need using up.

✱ Put the potatoes into a large pan, cover with water and boil for 15–20 minutes until soft. Drain and mash. Leave to cool.

✱ Mix the mashed potato with the tuna, breadcrumbs, ketchup, mayonnaise, sweetcorn, chives and Parmesan. Mix until blended, then shape into 16 little fish cakes. Coat each of them in the flour.

✱ Heat the oil in a frying pan then fry the fish cakes for 2 minutes each side until lightly golden. You may need to do this in batches.

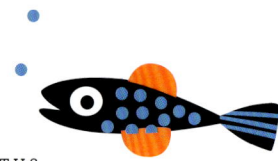

Salmon, squash and pea risotto

Suitable from 9 months
Makes 4-6 portions

Serving cooked rice with oily fish and vegetables is an ideal way to introduce texture to your baby's food whilst giving them all the necessary vitamins and minerals they need for a healthy diet. As a twist, try substituting the squash for pumpkin – yum!

✴ Heat the oil in a saucepan and fry the onion and squash for 5 minutes. Add the rice and stock. Bring up to the boil, cover and gently simmer for about 15 minutes until the rice is just cooked, then add the peas and cook until tender.

✴ Put the salmon and lemon juice into a bowl, cover with clingfilm and poke a few holes in it then cook for 2 minutes in the microwave on High. Flake the fish into the risotto and gently stir in the lemon juice. Sprinkle over the Parmesan and serve immediately.

Ingredients

1 tbsp olive oil
1 small onion, peeled and chopped
100g (4oz) butternut squash, peeled and diced
125g (4½oz) risotto rice
450ml (15 fl oz) unsalted fish stock
50g (2oz) frozen peas
200g (7oz) boneless, skinless salmon fillet, diced
Juice ½ lemon
25g (1oz) Parmesan, grated

Suitable from 12 months
Makes 6 kebabs

Marinated salmon kebabs

Ingredients

1 tbsp tomato ketchup
1 tbsp soy sauce
175g (6oz) boneless, skinless salmon fillet

6 small bamboo skewers soaked in water for 20 minutes

Forget fancy sauces, ketchup and soy sauce are the perfect combo to accompany my scrummy salmon kebabs. In fact, the whole family will love them, but remember to remove the skewers before serving to tots.

✶ Pre-heat the oven to 200C / 400F/ Gas 6.

✶ Mix the ketchup and soy together in a bowl. Cut the salmon into 24 cubes, coat in the ketchup and soy and set aside to marinate for 10 minutes.

✶ Thread the salmon cubes onto skewers and place them on a baking tray. Bake in the oven for 8 minutes until cooked through.

✶ Allow to cool a little, then remove the fish from the skewers and serve with vegetables as finger food.

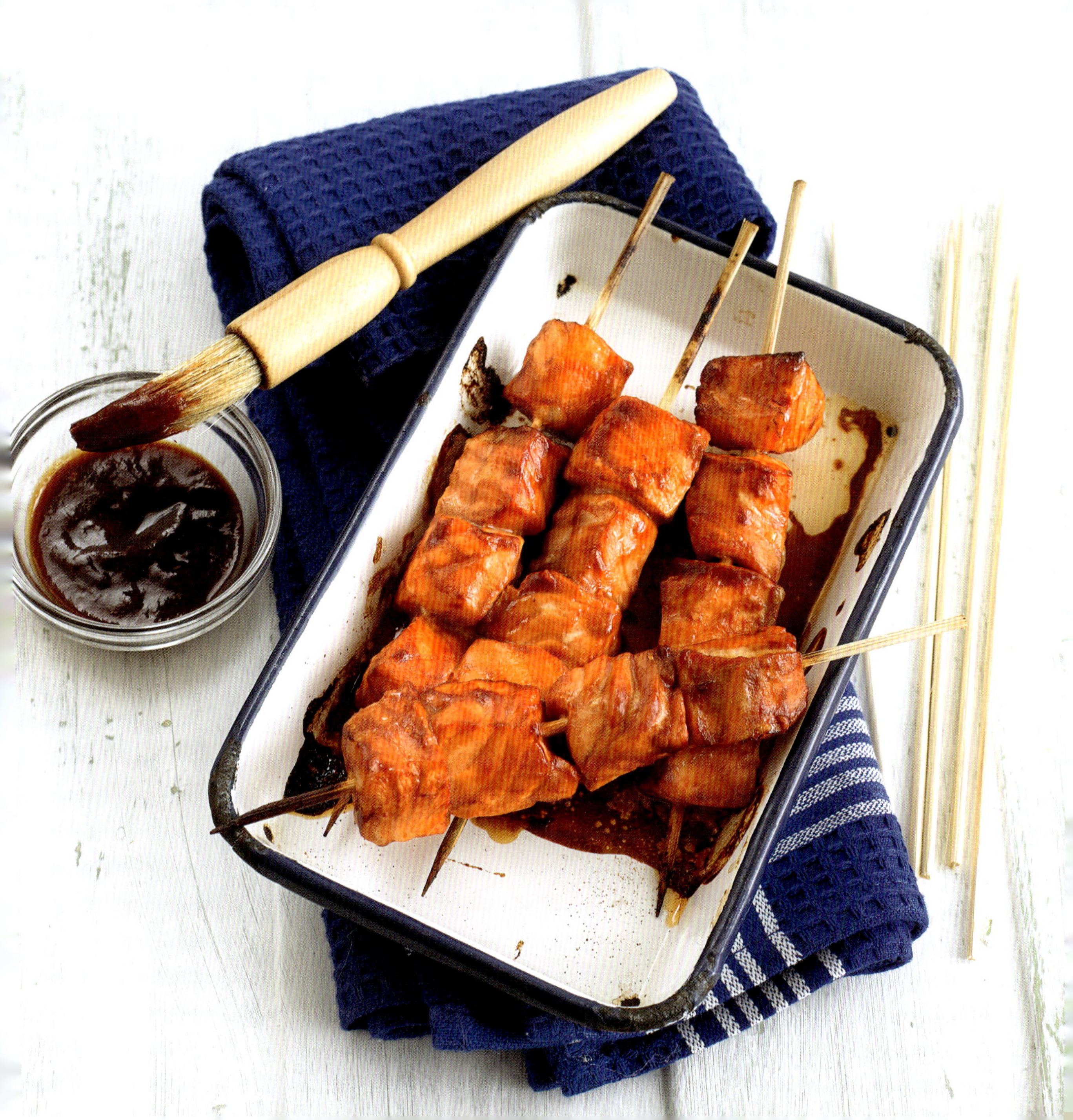

Suitable from 9 months
Makes 9 nuggets

Salmon nuggets

Ingredients

150g (5oz) boneless, skinless salmon fillet
15g (½oz) cornflakes
10g (½oz) Parmesan, finely grated
¼ tsp grated lemon zest
1 small egg, beaten

Believe it or not, crushed-up cornflakes make a tasty coating for fish. My bite-sized salmon nuggets crisp up beautifully when baked, and they are so quick to make. Rice Krispies are another winner when it comes to healthy coatings – it's great to experiment.

✱ Pre-heat the oven to 200C /400F / Gas 6.

✱ Cut the salmon into 2cm (1in) cubes. Put the cornflakes into a polythene bag and bash them with a rolling pin until finely crushed. Add the cheese and lemon zest to the crushed cornflakes.

✱ Put the beaten egg in a shallow bowl then dip the salmon cubes into the egg, then add them to the bag. Gently shake until all the cubes are coated with the cornflakes.

✱ Place the cubes on a baking sheet lined with non-stick paper and bake in the oven for 10 minutes until golden.

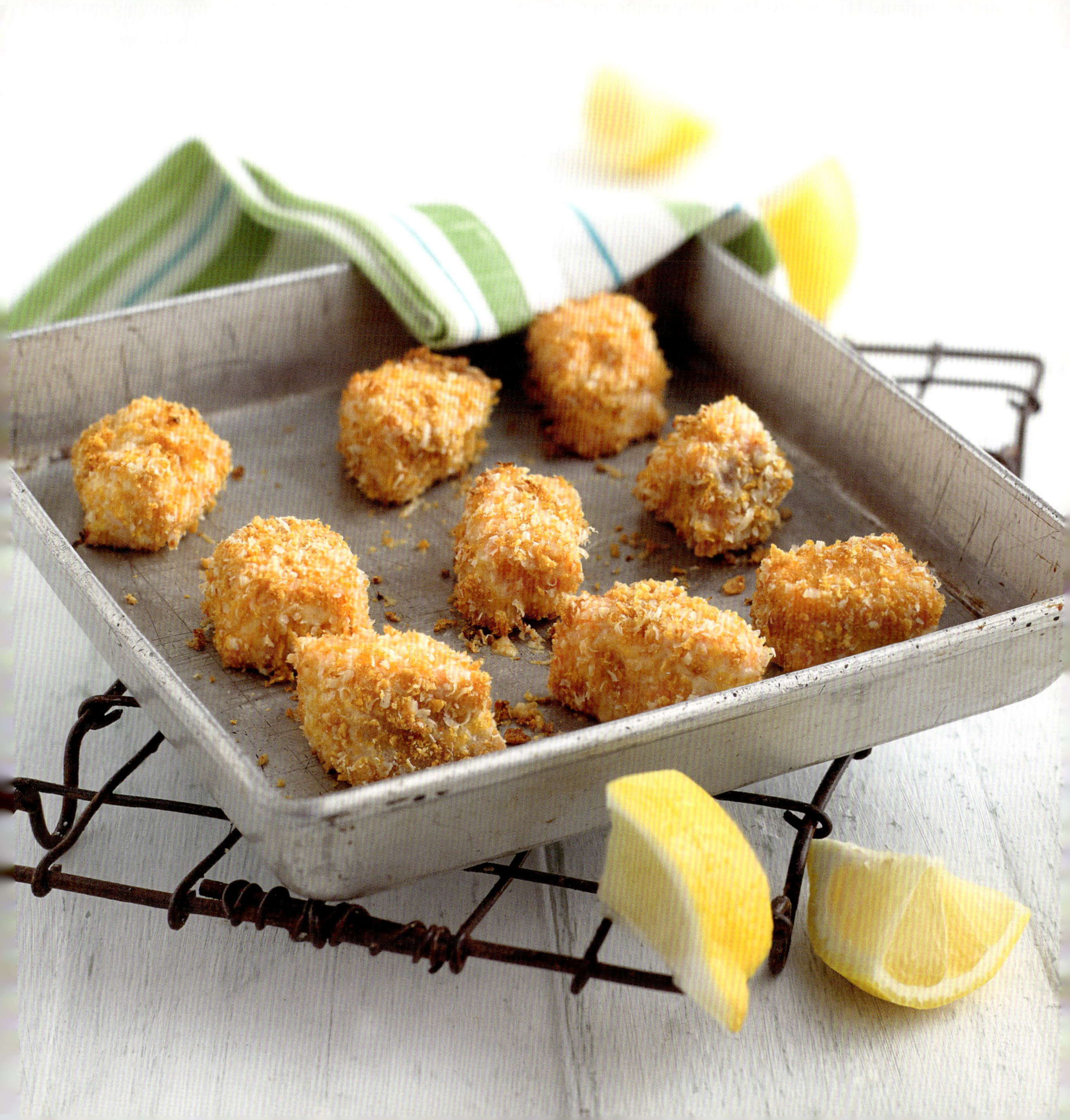

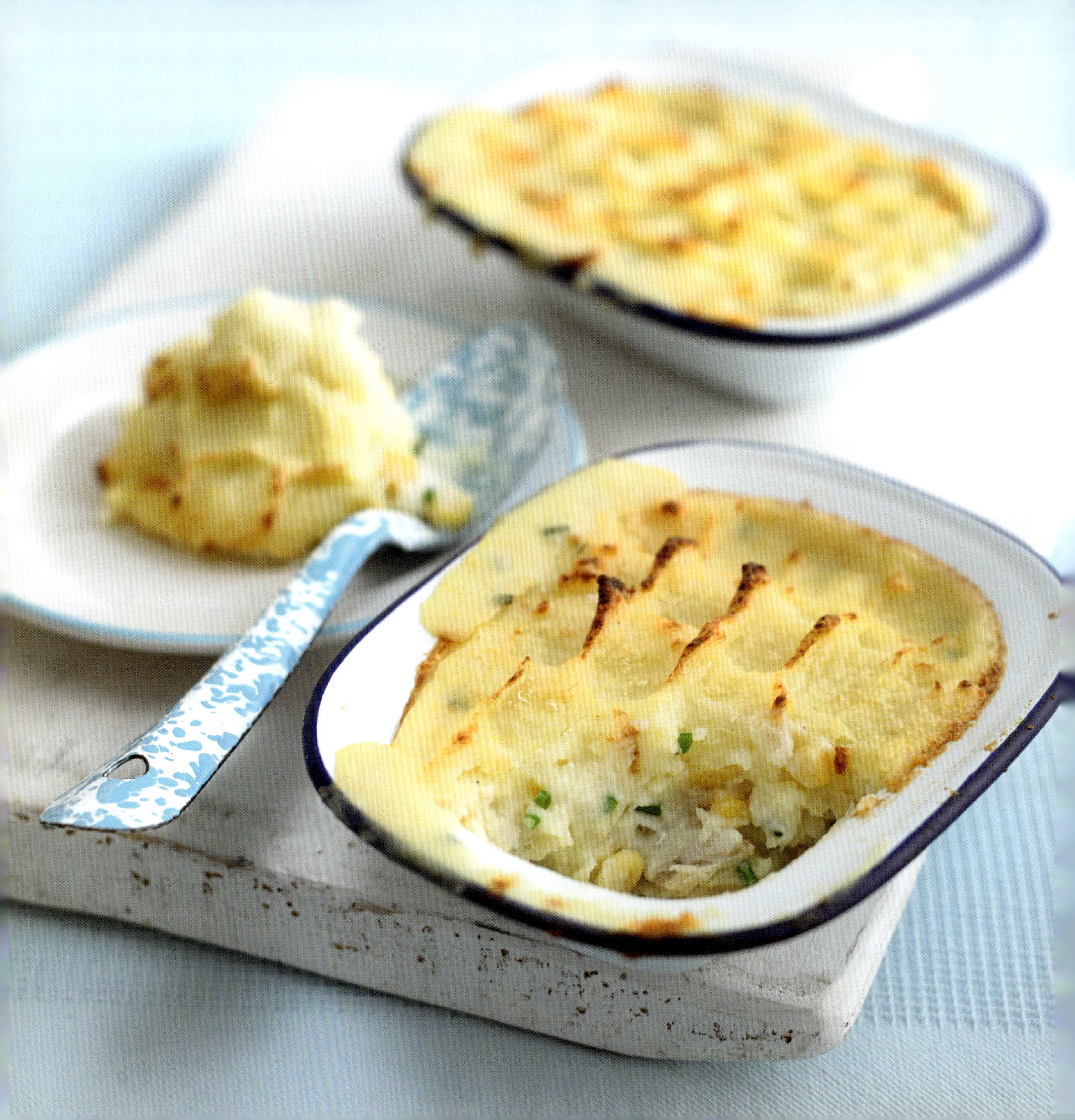

Cod and sweetcorn fish pies

Suitable for freezing
Suitable from 9 months
Makes 4 portions

If you want your child to grow up enjoying fish then try this super scrumptious pie, which is simple to prepare. If you make these in ramekin dishes they will be just the right size for your little one to enjoy – too much food in front of them can be a little daunting. It is a good idea to keep a stock of these mini fish pies in the freezer for those extra busy days.

∗ Put the potatoes into a large pan and cover with cold water. Boil for 15–20 minutes until soft. Drain, then mash with a knob of butter and a little milk. Set aside.

∗ Pre-heat the oven to 200C / 400F / Gas 6.

∗ Melt the butter in a saucepan, then fry the onion for 5 minutes until soft. Add the flour and then whisk in the milk to make a smooth sauce. Bring to the boil and simmer for 2 minutes, then add the cheese and chives, stir in, then add the cod and sweetcorn.

∗ Spoon the fish mixture into 4 ramekins and top with the mashed potato. Bake in the oven for 15 minutes until lightly golden and bubbling.

Ingredients

450g (1lb) white potatoes, peeled and chopped
20g (1oz) butter, plus extra for the mash
1 small onion, peeled and chopped
3 tbsp plain flour
250ml (9fl oz) milk, plus extra for the mash
40g (1½oz) Cheddar cheese, grated
1 tsp snipped chives
150g (5oz) boneless, skinless cod fillet, diced
2 tbsp sweetcorn, frozen or canned

Suitable for freezing
Suitable from 12 months
Makes 20 meatballs

Beef

Sticky meatballs

Meatballs
225g (8oz) minced beef
25g (1oz) Parmesan, grated
1 tsp dried thyme
50g (2oz) breadcrumbs
1 egg yolk

Sauce
Juice of 1 orange
3 tbsp tomato ketchup
1 tbsp honey
1 tsp Worcestershire sauce
2 tsp soy sauce

My sticky meatballs are mini in size, but mighty in flavour – especially when coated with my unique sauce. Serve with a portion of their favourite veg and your little ones will be stuck on these. If you want to freeze them, it's best to freeze them uncooked on a tray lined with clingfilm. When frozen, wrap each one individually in clingfilm so that you can remove and defrost them as you need them.

✶ Pre-heat the oven to 200C / 400F / Gas 6.

✶ Put all of the meatball ingredients into a bowl and combine. With damp hands, divide and shape the mixture into 20 balls. Place the balls on a baking sheet and bake in the oven for 12 minutes until golden and cooked through.

✶ While the meatballs are cooking, measure all of the sauce ingredients into a large saucepan. Heat gently and stir until syrupy, then add the meatballs and coat them all in the sauce.

Mini beef burgers

Fast, tasty food doesn't have to be unhealthy. Homemade burgers are better than any you'll buy – my secret is adding Worcestershire sauce and apple for a sweet, tangy flavour.

Ingredients

1 onion, peeled
¼ red pepper, deseeded
½ dessert apple, peeled
25g (1oz) breadcrumbs
1 tsp chopped fresh thyme
225g (8oz) minced beef
45g (1½oz) Cheddar, grated
A few drops Worcestershire sauce
Olive oil, for frying

✶ Put the onion, pepper and apple into a food processor and blend until chopped. Add the breadcrumbs, thyme, beef, Cheddar and Worcestershire sauce and whiz briefly until combined. With damp hands, divide and shape the mixture into 16 burgers.

✶ Heat a little oil in a large frying pan and fry the burgers for 5–8 minutes until golden and cooked through. You may need to cook them in batches.

Suitable for freezing
Suitable from 9 months
Makes 16 burgers

Beef with sweet pepper

Beyond six months it is especially important to give your baby iron-rich food. Red meat such as lean minced beef is a great starting place – especially when combined with tantalising flavours such as smoked paprika.

Ingredients

1 tsp olive oil
1 onion, peeled and chopped
85g (3oz) red pepper, deseeded and diced
100g (4oz) sweet potato, peeled and diced
½ clove garlic, crushed
125g (4½oz) minced beef
85g (3oz) mushrooms, chopped
¼ tsp sweet smoked paprika
150g (5oz) tomato passata
200ml (7fl oz) water

✶ Heat the oil in a saucepan and fry the onion, pepper, potato and garlic for 1 minute. Add the beef and mushrooms and brown over the heat. Add the paprika, passata and water and simmer everything together for 20 minutes until tender. Blend to a chunky consistency.

Suitable for freezing
Suitable from 9 months
Makes 3 portions

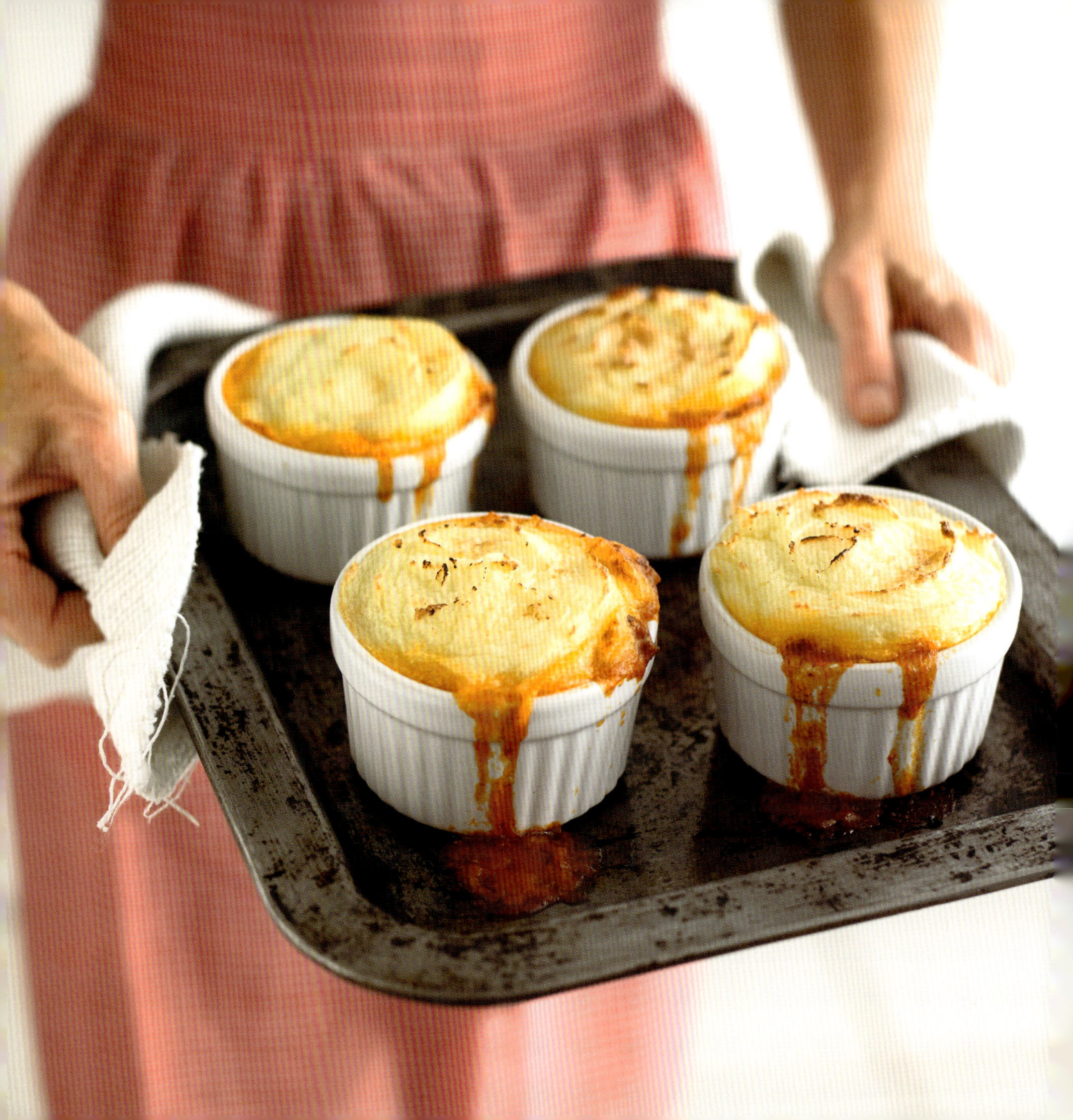

Mini cottage pies

Suitable for freezing, assembled and uncooked
Suitable from 9 months
Makes 4 portions

Growing up, my son Nicholas was a very fussy eater, but I always won him over with my homemade cottage pie – especially as I could cleverly disguise the extra veg inside.

★ Pre-heat the oven to 200C / 400F / Gas 6.

★ Put the potatoes in a large pan, cover with water, then boil for 15–20 minutes until soft. Drain and mash with the butter and milk.

★ Put the oil into a saucepan and fry the onion, carrot and celery for 5 minutes. Add the beef and fry until browned. Add the flour, then blend in the stock, purée, thyme, Worcestershire sauce and bay leaf. Cover and simmer gently for 20 minutes.

★ Remove the bay leaf and spoon the mixture into 4 ramekins (each approx 10cm/4in in diameter). Spread the mash on top and fork it over to create a pattern. Bake in the oven for 15 minutes until the meat is bubbling and the top is brown.

Ingredients

500g (1lb 2oz) potatoes, peeled and diced
A knob of butter
A little milk
1 tbsp olive oil
½ onion, peeled and finely chopped
1 small carrot, peeled and diced
1 stick celery, diced
150g (5oz) lean minced beef
2 tbsp plain flour
250ml (9fl oz) weak unsalted beef stock
1 tsp tomato purée
1 tsp chopped fresh thyme
A few drops Worcestershire sauce
1 bay leaf

Suitable from 12 months
Makes 4 portions

First beef noodle stir-fry

Stir-fry
75g (3oz) carrot, peeled and diced
75g (3oz) egg noodles
50g (2oz) frozen peas
2 tsp sunflower oil
100g (4oz) sirloin steak

Sauce
4 spring onions, finely sliced
½ clove garlic, crushed
3 tbsp pure, unsweetened apple juice
1 tbsp soy sauce
½ tsp caster sugar

Full of colour, flavour and goodness, a stir-fry takes minutes to make and it's a great way to get your little one to eat more vegetables. Here is a tasty wok recipe that will rock your little one's high chair.

✱ Put the diced carrot into a small saucepan and cover with water. Bring up to the boil and cook for 5 minutes. Add the noodles and peas to the pan and boil for 5 minutes. Drain everything and chop up the noodles into tiny pieces using a knife and fork.

✱ Heat the oil in a frying pan. Bash out the steak thinly, then slice into tiny strips. Fry the beef for 2 minutes until cooked through. Add the noodles and vegetables to the pan.

✱ Mix all of the sauce ingredients together in a small bowl. Pour the sauce over the noodles and toss everything together over the heat for 1 minute. Serve straight away.

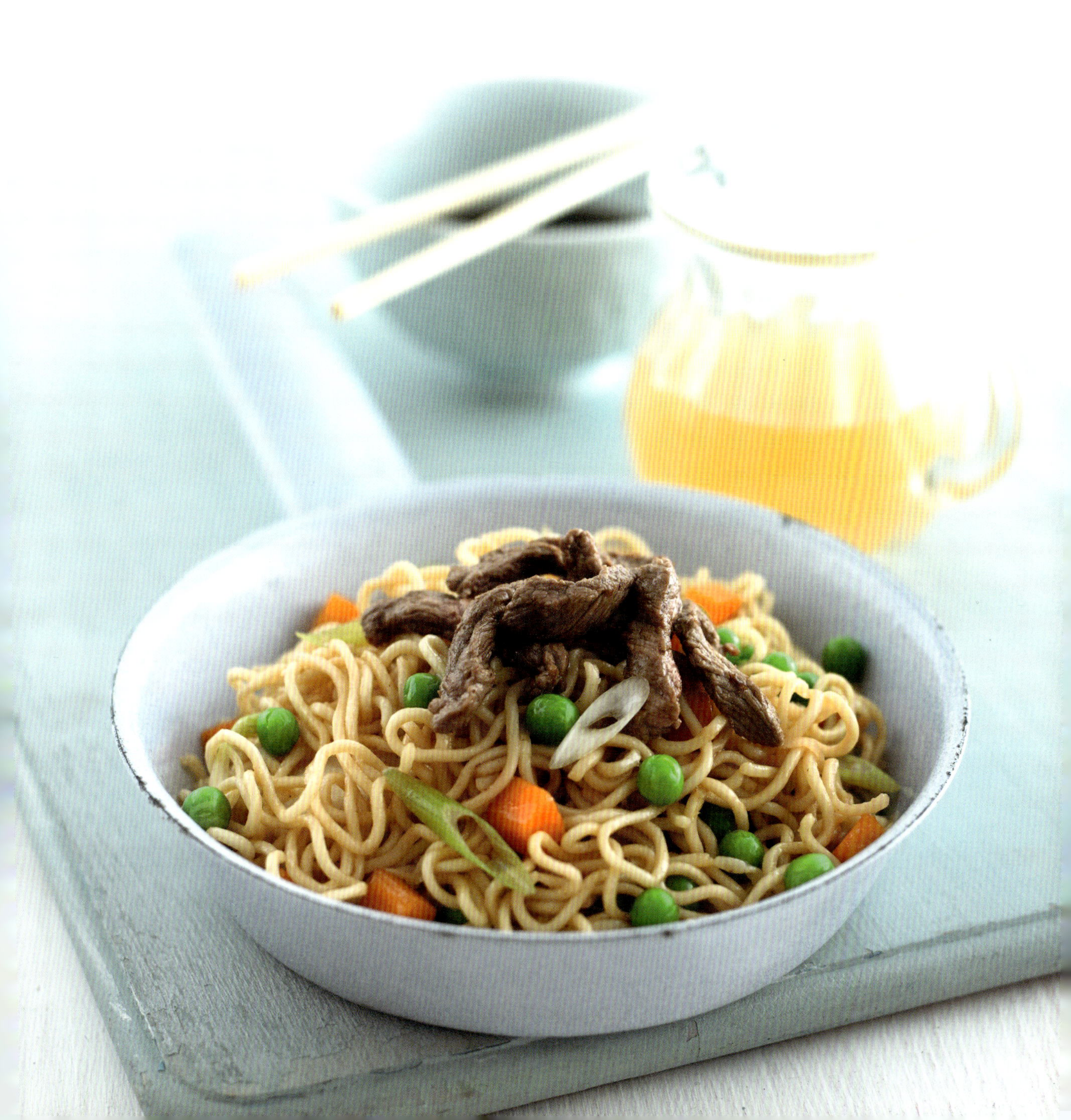

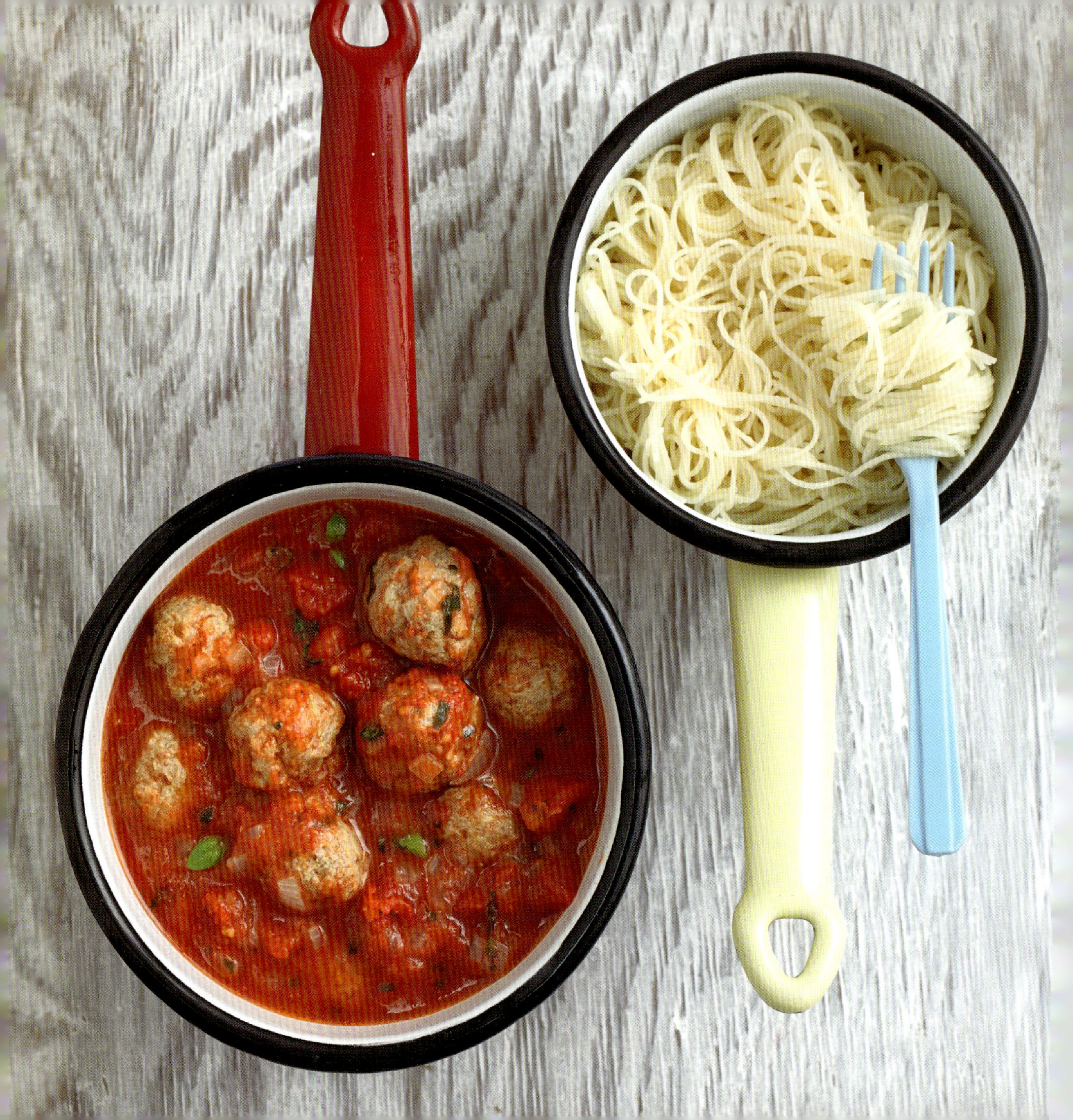

Meatballs in tomato sauce

Suitable for freezing
Suitable from 9 months
Makes 20 meatballs

Meatballs are magnificent! They're perfect with my quick-and-easy homemade tomato sauce. You could even make these with pork or turkey mince. These meatballs also make good finger food without the sauce. If you want to freeze them, do so as for Mini Beef Burgers (page 147).

★ Put all the meatball ingredients into a bowl and combine. With damp hands, shape the mixture into 20 balls.

★ For the tomato sauce, heat the oil in a saucepan and fry the onion for 5 minutes until soft. Add the garlic and cook for 30 seconds. Add the remaining ingredients and bring everything up to the boil. Drop in the meatballs, cover with a lid and simmer for 15 minutes until cooked through.

Meatballs

225g (8oz) minced beef
1 tsp chopped fresh thyme
25g (1oz) Parmesan, grated
50g (2oz) breadcrumbs
1 egg yolk

Tomato sauce

1 tbsp olive oil
1 onion, peeled and chopped
1 clove garlic, crushed
400g can chopped tomatoes
100ml (3½fl oz) water
1 tbsp tomato purée
1 tsp chopped fresh thyme
1 tbsp chopped fresh basil

Finger foods

Sandwiches

Suitable from 9 months. Makes 2 round or 4 finger sandwiches

There's no doubt about it – we love sandwiches. They're quick to make, they keep well, and everyone can eat them. But it's also easy to get into a sandwich rut, reaching for the same failsafe fillings day in and day out.

Sometimes we all need a little inspiration to shake up our sandwich routine, so here are some of my tried-and-tested favourites.

Cream cheese and jam

Coming up with something different doesn't have to be about reinventing the wheel. Cheese and jam are favourites of their own, but combining them creates a whole new sweet and creamy taste experience – my children loved it.

Ingredients
A knob of butter
2 slices white bread
1 tbsp cream cheese
1½ tsp low-sugar strawberry jam

✴ Lightly butter one side of each slice of bread. Spread the cream cheese over the other slice. Spread jam on the buttered side, then sandwich together. Remove the crusts and slice into 6 fingers or cut into circles, removing a circle window from the top slice with a smaller cutter.

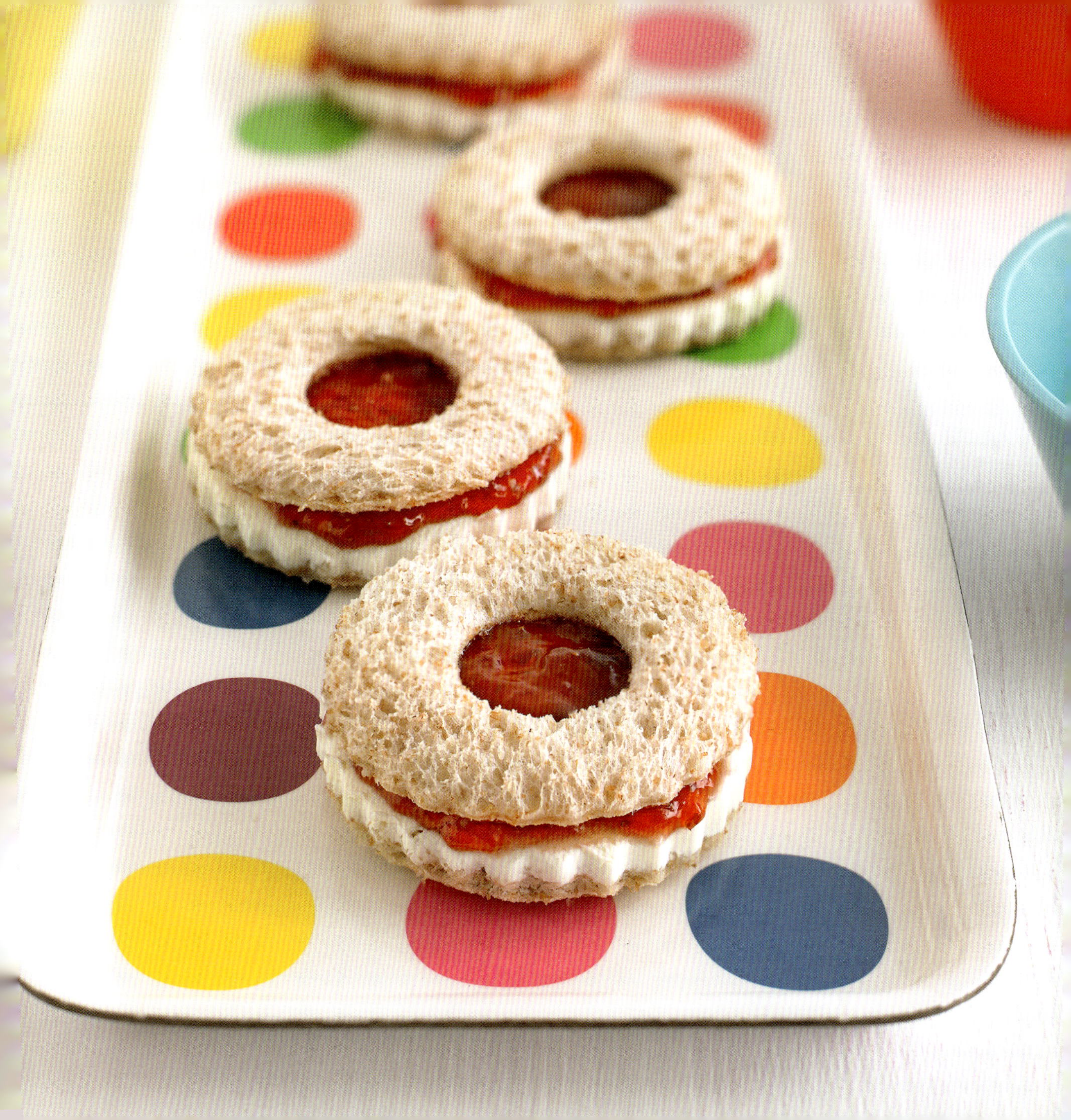

Suitable from 9 months
Makes 6 mini sandwiches

Chicken, tomato and cheese

This is a really quick and easy way of giving your child plenty of protein without any fuss. Simply save some chicken from an evening meal (it might have been that Sunday roast), then use it as a sandwich filler. Leave adding the tomato until the last moment.

Ingredients

50g (2oz) cooked chicken, diced
½ tomato, deseeded and diced
1 tsp snipped chives
1 tbsp light mayonnaise
1 tbsp grated Cheddar cheese
A knob of butter
2 slices brown bread

✶ Mix the chicken, tomato, chives, mayonnaise and Cheddar together. Lightly butter one slice of bread, then sandwich the two slices together. Remove the crusts and slice into 6 fingers.

Suitable from 9 months
Makes 6 mini sandwiches

Cream cheese, sweet chilli and cucumber

Sweet chilli is a great flavour to introduce to your child in a sandwich as it fuses perfectly with the light, creamy cheese. A quick tip; using a thin spread of butter will prevent the bread from going soggy.

Ingredients

A knob of butter
2 slices white bread
1 tbsp cream cheese
1½ tsp sweet chilli sauce
6 slices cucumber

✶ Lightly butter one side of each slice of bread. Spread the cream cheese over the other slice. Spread the sweet chilli sauce over the buttered slice and top with the cucumber. Sandwich together, remove the crusts and slice into 6 fingers.

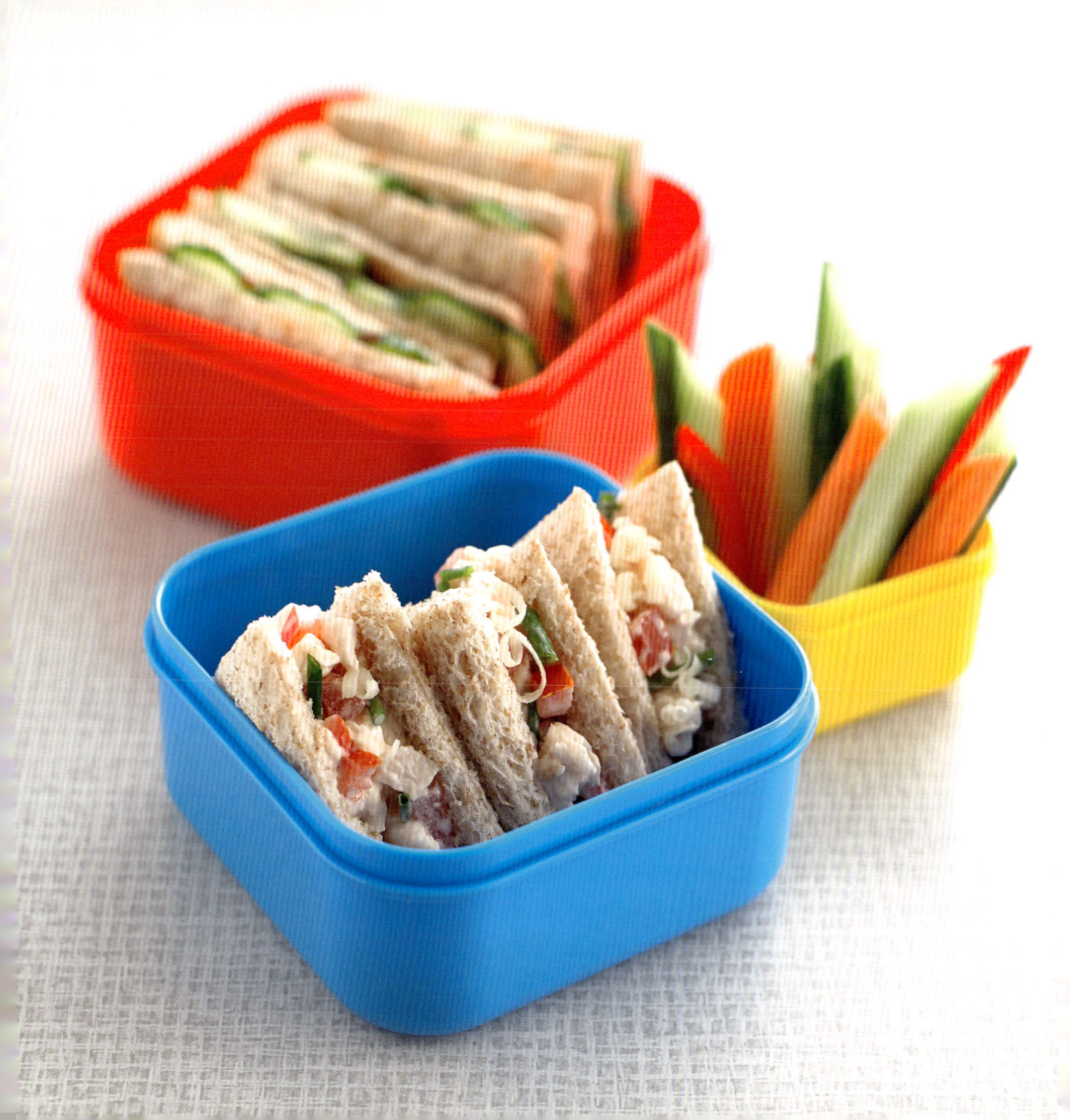

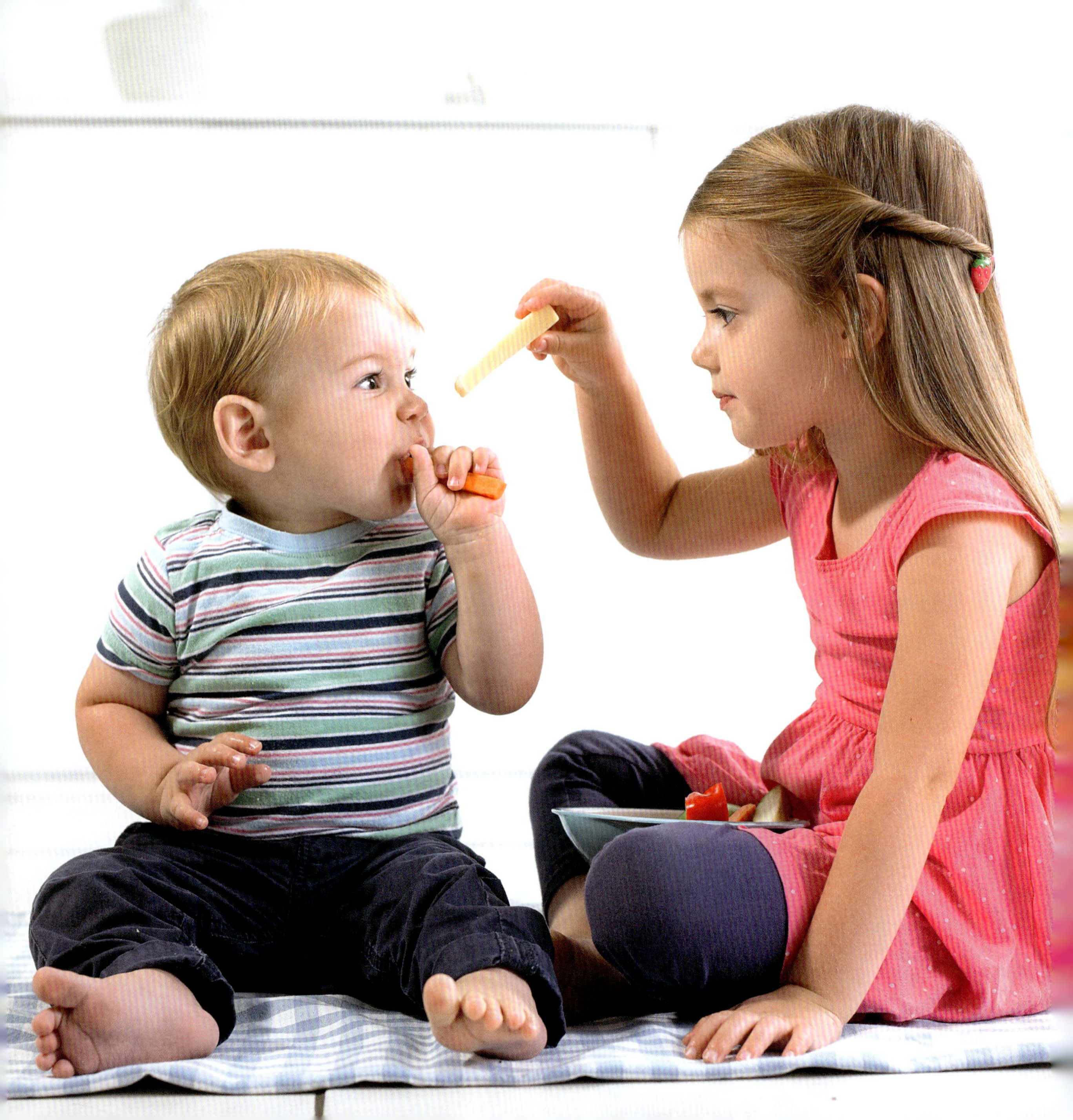

Egg mayo and tomato pinwheels

Step aside sandwiches, my tortilla-based pinwheels are the new lunchtime treat in town. I love the creamy taste of egg mayo with juicy tomato, but you can roll up any of their favourite fillers in quick-time.

Ingredients

1 mini tortilla wrap
1 egg
1 tbsp mayonnaise
½ tomato, deseeded and diced
1 tsp snipped chives

✱ Warm the tortilla in the microwave for 30 seconds on High.

✱ Cook the egg in a pan of boiling water for 10 minutes. Run it under cold water to stop it cooking and to cool the shell, then peel it and mash the egg in a bowl. Add the mayonnaise, tomato and chives.

✱ Spread the mixture over the wrap, then roll it up and slice into 8 pinwheels.

Suitable from 12 months. Makes 2 portions

Ham and cream cheese pinwheels

Children are naturally inquisitive, and this pinwheel recipe is another great way of encouraging them to experiment with their favourite fillers.

Ingredients

1 mini tortilla wrap
2 tsp cream cheese
1 slice ham, chopped

✱ Warm the tortilla in the microwave for 30 seconds on High.

✱ Spread the cream cheese and ham over the wrap, then roll it up and slice into 8 pinwheels.

Suitable from 12 months. Makes 2 portions

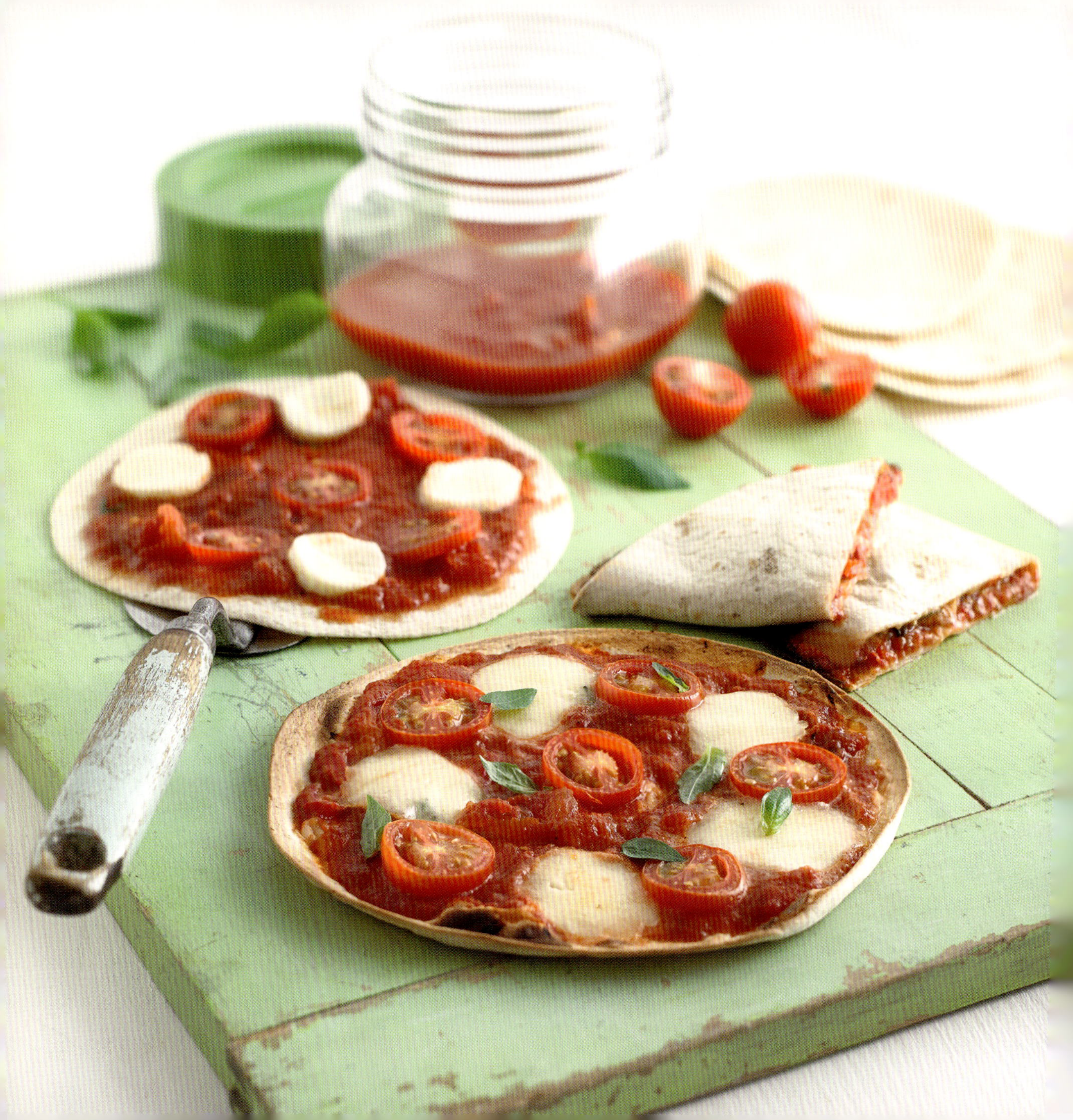

Tortilla pizza wedges

Suitable from 9 months
Makes 4 pizzas

Kids want 'fun' stuff to eat. You want to provide healthy food that will fuel them through the day. My simple and quick pizza wedges are utterly delicious and travel remarkably well. Kids and adults will love them.

★ Pre-heat the grill to hot. Arrange two wraps on two baking sheets.

★ Mix together the tomatoes, sundried tomato paste, sugar and basil in a small bowl. Spread the sauce over the wraps. Top each with the cherry tomatoes and mozzarella cheese. Grill the pizzas for 5–8 minutes until the cheese is melted and golden and the wraps are crisp around the edges. Slice into wedges.

Ingredients

4 mini tortilla wraps
6 tbsp chopped tomatoes, from a can
2 tbsp sundried tomato paste
Pinch of sugar
2 tbsp chopped fresh basil
8 cherry tomatoes, sliced
100g (4oz) mozzarella, sliced

Suitable for freezing
Suitable from 9 months
Makes 4 portions

Nectarine, apple and blueberry compote

Ingredients

A knob of butter
1 nectarine, stoned and diced
1 dessert apple, peeled, cored and diced
1 tsp caster sugar
100g (4oz) blueberries
2 tbsp pure, unsweetened apple juice

Blueberries are a superfood as they are packed with a host of amazing nutrients. They are great as a snack, but even better when mixed into a fruity compote and stirred into porridge or whipped up with yogurt.

✱ Melt the butter in a saucepan, add the nectarine, apple and sugar and simmer for 3–4 minutes. Add the blueberries and apple juice and continue to simmer for 3 minutes until soft.

Plum, pear and apple porridge

Suitable from 9 months
Makes 2 portions

This recipe brings a fruity burst to ordinary porridge. This fruit trio works wonderfully, but you could use all kinds of fruit that are in season, or even buy frozen fruit, which still contains those all-important nutrients.

✶ Put the plums, pear, apples and apple juice into a saucepan and simmer for 5–7 minutes until the fruit is soft.

✶ In another pan, heat the milk. Add the cranberries and porridge oats and cook, stirring, for 3 minutes. Mix the fruit into the porridge and blend everything until smooth.

Ingredients

2 plums, chopped
1 pear, peeled, cored and diced
2 dessert apples, peeled, cored and diced
2 tbsp pure, unsweetened apple juice
150ml (5fl oz) milk
20g (1oz) dried cranberries
20g (1oz) porridge oats

Suitable from 9 months
Makes 8 lollies

Berry and yogurt ice lollies

Ingredients

150g (5oz) blueberries
100g (4oz) raspberries
200g (7oz) strawberries, hulled and quartered
60–75g (2½–3oz) caster sugar
2 x 100g pots blueberry Actimel

Ice lollies are very refreshing for toddlers, and are perfect for helping to soothe teething gums. You could use a variety of different fruits including mango, pear and strawberry, but don't forget to choose a yogurt that is low in sugar.

✱ Measure the fruit into a small saucepan with the sugar and cook over a medium heat, stirring, until liquid has come out of the fruits, then lower the heat and simmer for 4 minutes until the fruit has softened. Leave to cool then blend until smooth.

✱ Tip the cooled fruit into a sieve set over a jug. Add the yogurts and a little more sugar to the strained fruit if they are sharp. Pour the mixture into 8 lolly moulds and freeze overnight.

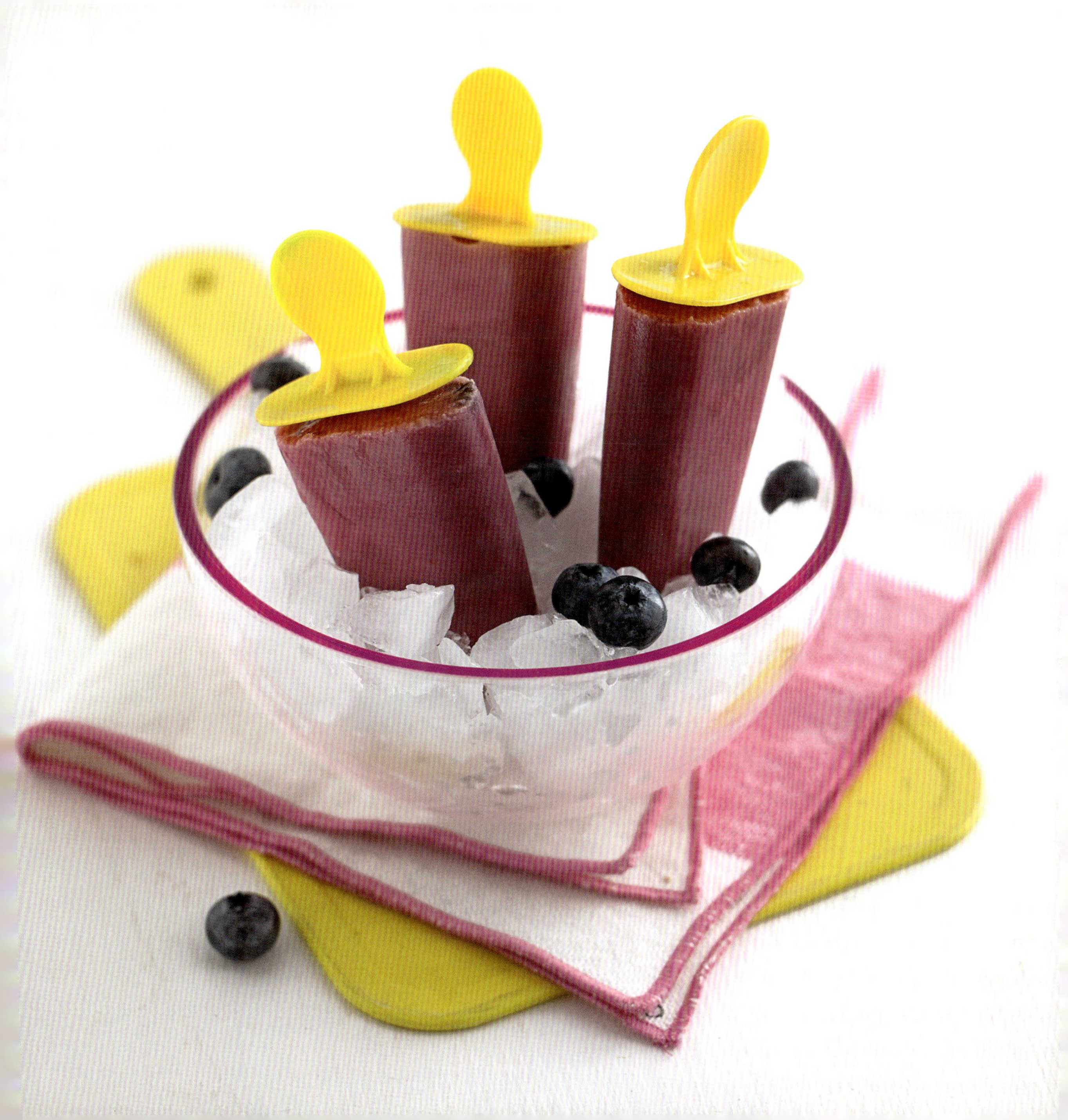

Suitable for freezing
Suitable from 9 months
Makes 4 individual crumbles

Pear, apple and blueberry crumbles

Fruit

A knob of butter
2 pears, peeled, cored and diced
2 dessert apples, peeled, cored and diced
50g (2oz) caster sugar
150g (5oz) blueberries

Crumble topping

150g (5oz) plain flour
65g (2½oz) butter
25g (1oz) brown sugar

This healthy crumble is full of antioxidants from the blueberries and fibre from the pear and apple. With my delicious golden crispy topping, it's an easy way to get your child eating – and enjoying – more fruit.

★ Pre-heat the oven to 200C / 400F / Gas 6.

★ Melt the butter in a small pan, add the pears, apples and sugar and simmer for 3–4 minutes. Add the blueberries, stir through and remove from the heat. Spoon the fruits into 4 ovenproof ramekins or teacups.

★ Measure the flour, butter and brown sugar for the crumble topping into a bowl and rub it together with your fingertips until it looks like breadcrumbs. Sprinkle this crumble mix on top of the fruits. Bake the crumbles in the oven for 15–20 minutes until the topping is browning and the fruits are bubbling.

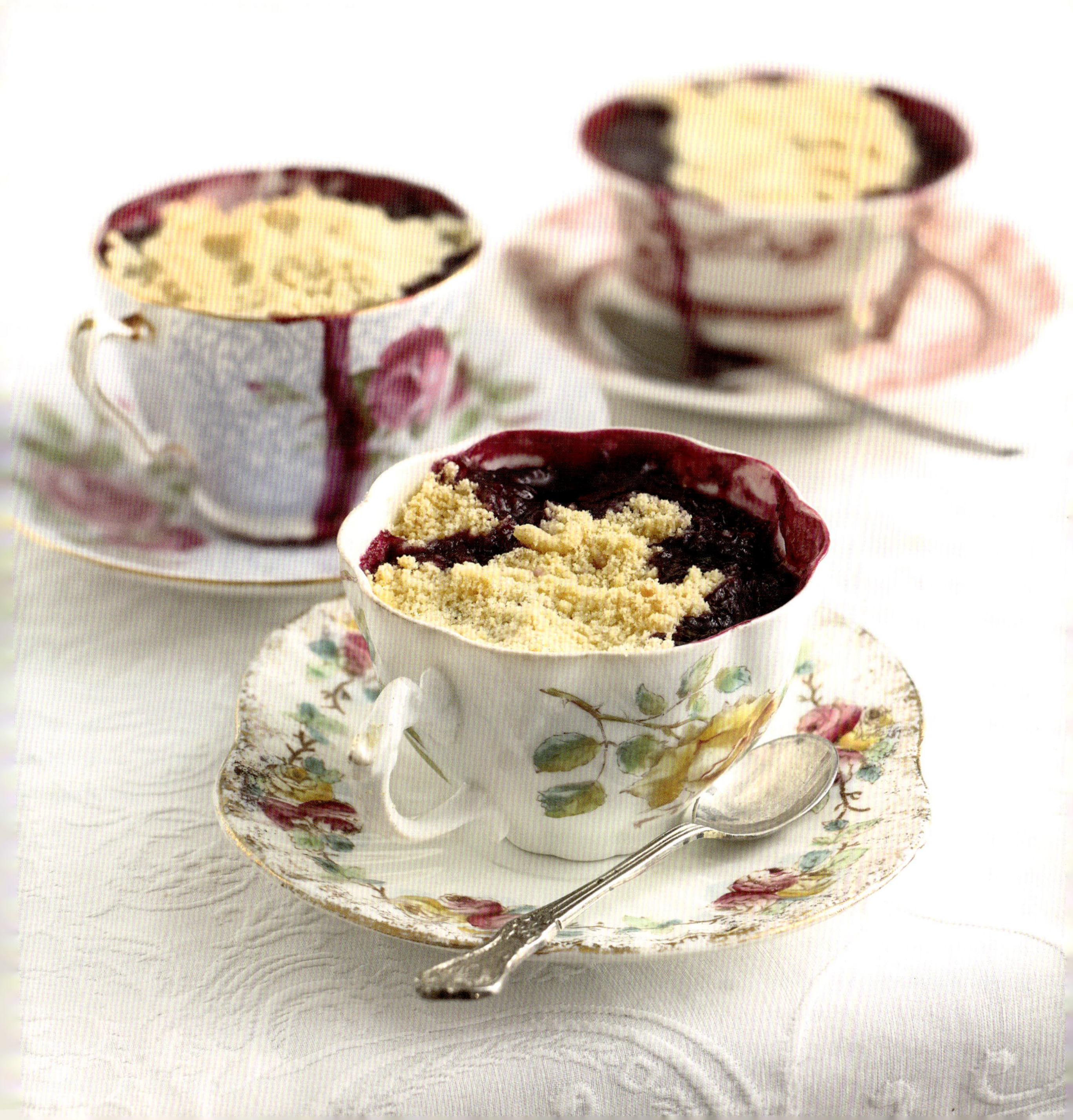

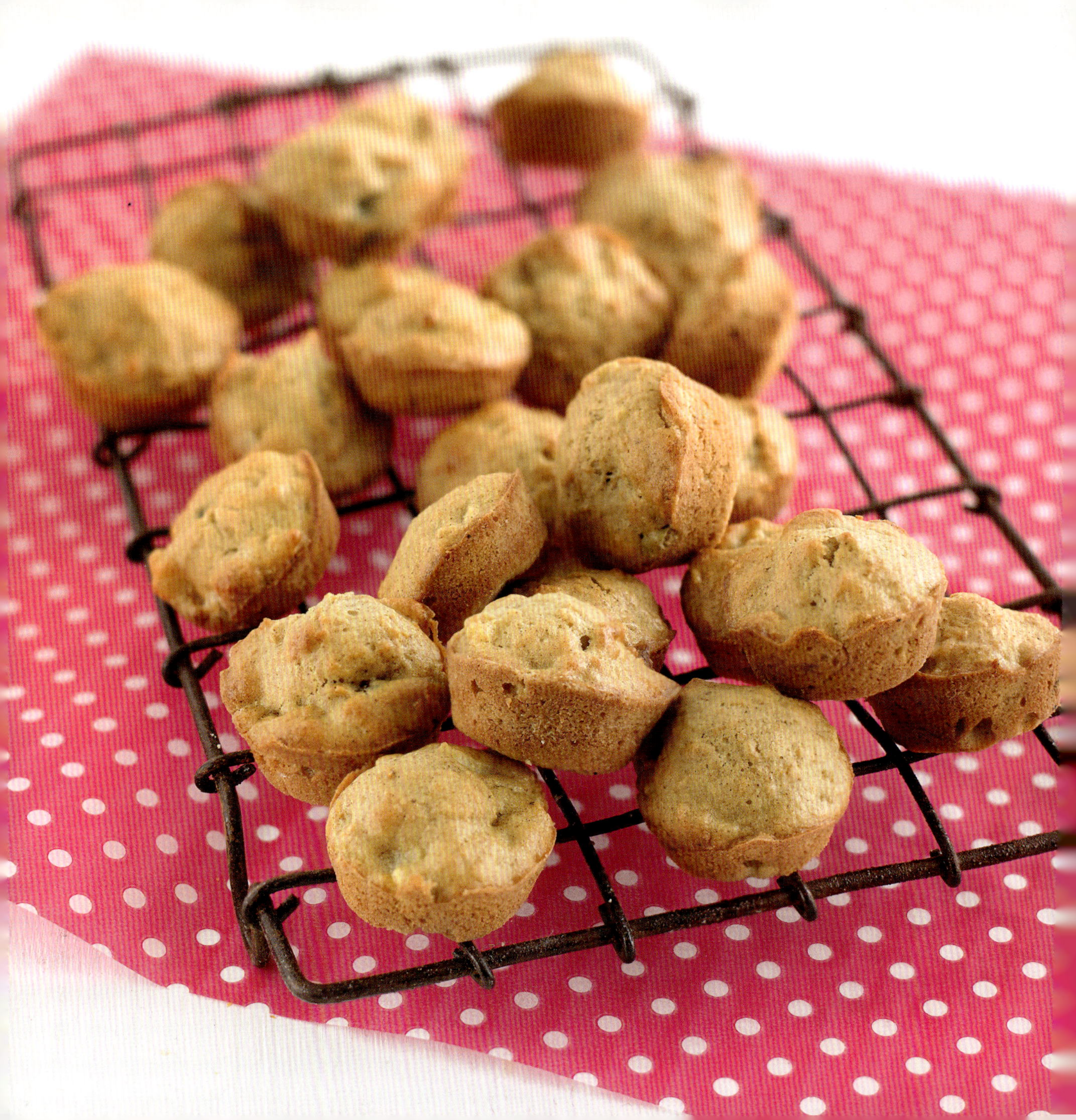

Sweet potato and apple mini muffins

Suitable from 9 months
Makes 24 mini muffins

Adding sweet root vegetables to a traditional muffin recipe really does work! These sweet potato muffins are nutritious, delicious and easy to prepare. As well as making a perfect finger food for babies, they are ideal for the whole family.

✱ Pre-heat the oven to 200C/ 400F / Gas 6. Line a 24-hole mini-muffin tin with paper cases.

✱ Measure all of the ingredients into a large bowl and blend until smooth using an electric hand whisk. Spoon the mixture into the cases.

✱ Bake in the oven for 15 minutes until well risen and lightly golden. Cool for 5 minutes in the tin then transfer to a wire rack to cool completely.

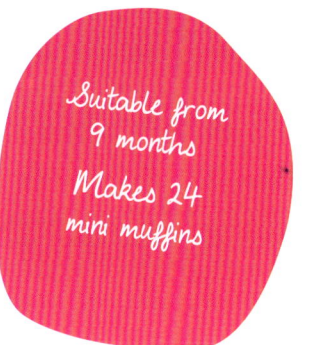

Ingredients

150g (5oz) plain flour
75g (3oz) caster sugar
½ tsp ground cinnamon
½ tsp ground ginger
50ml (2fl oz) sunflower oil
75g (3oz) apple sauce
½ tsp vanilla extract
1 tsp baking powder
50g (2oz) raisins
½ dessert apple, peeled and grated
50g (2oz) sweet potato, peeled and grated
1 egg

Suitable from 9 months
Makes 18 rusks

Spiced sultana rusks

Ingredients

50g (2oz) butter, softened
50g (2oz) soft brown sugar
1 egg
150g (5oz) plain flour, plus extra for dusting
1 tsp baking powder
1 tsp ground cinnamon
1 tsp ground ginger
25g (1oz) sultanas, chopped

Adding a little spice to a bland biscuit will make it far more interesting and inviting to your little one. It's easy to make your own rusks and they will keep for several weeks in an airtight container.

★ Pre-heat the oven to 180C / 350F / Gas 4.

★ Cream the butter and sugar together in a bowl. Add the egg, flour, baking powder, spices and sultanas and stir everything together. Tip the mixture out onto a floured work surface and lightly knead into a dough.

★ Divide the mixture into two, then roll out to 2 x 18 x 4cm (7 x 2in) sausage shapes.

★ Place on a baking sheet lined with baking paper and cook in the oven for 20–25 minutes. Remove from the oven and slice each sausage into 2cm (1in) thick slices. Put back into the oven for another 20 minutes, turning them all over halfway through the cooking time.

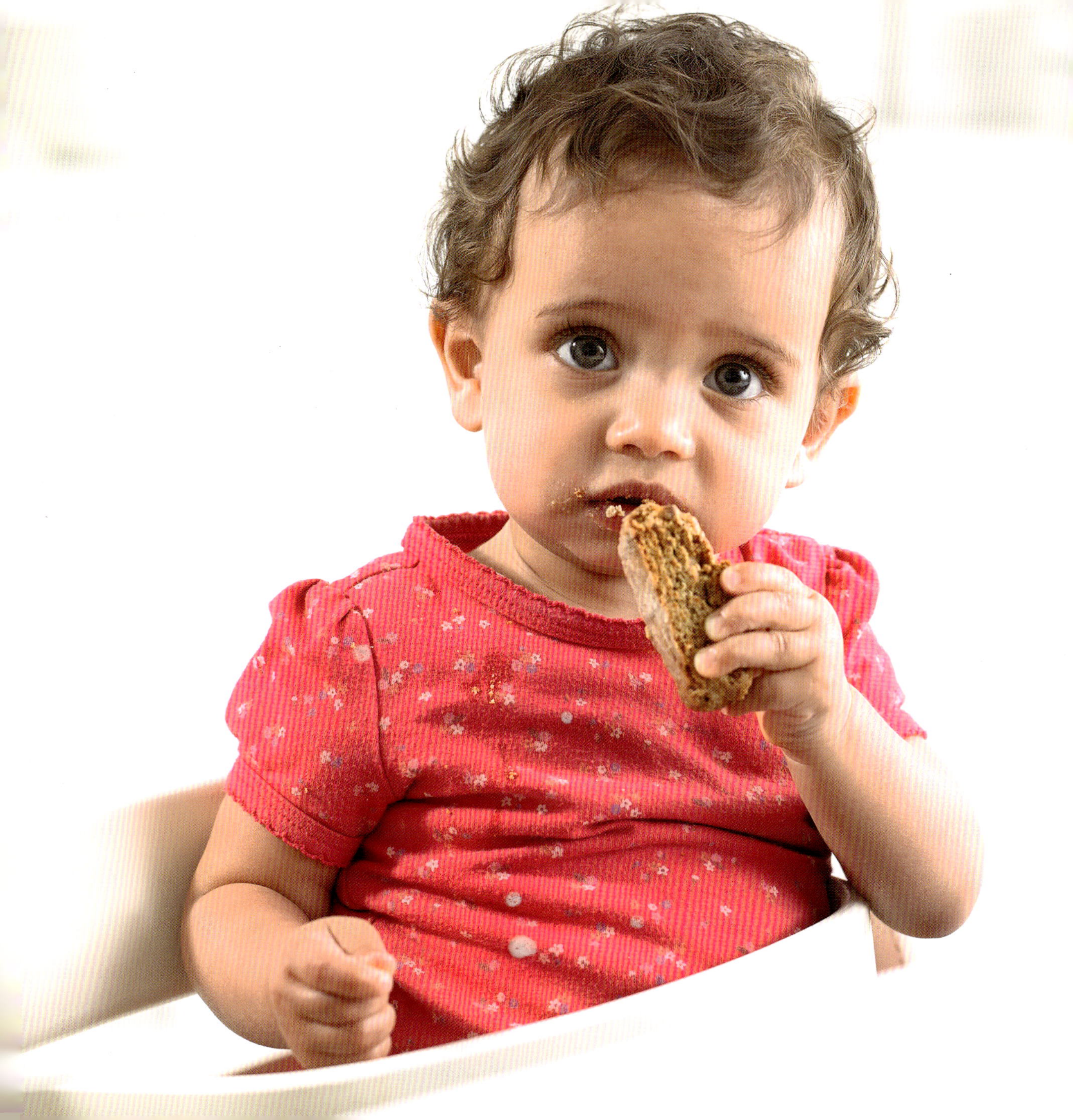

Index

anaphylaxis 10, 12
appetite 56
apple 18–19
    blueberry & nectarine 162
    & carrot 46
    carrot & parsnip 46
    & mango 38–9
    & nectarine 92
    & parsnip 45
    peach & blueberry 41
    & pear 20
    pear & apricot porridge 92
    pear & blueberry crumbles 166–7
    pear & raisin 36
    plum & pear porridge 163
    prune, squash & parsnip 44
    spinach & carrot 63
    spinach & swede 41
    & strawberry 36–7
    & sweet potato muffins 168–9
apricot
    apple & pear porridge 92
    banana & porridge 93
    & pear 93
    squash & carrot 42
    squash & chicken 80–1
aubergine 60, 116
avocado 8, 9, 28–9

banana 8, 9, 24
    apricot & porridge 93
    & avocado 29
    & blueberry 20
    blueberry & pear 90–1
    & mango 26
    & peach 24–5
    peach & strawberry 26–7
batch cooking 12
beef 54, 146–53
    Bolognese 88–9
    carrots & peas 84

casseroles 82, 84
    lentils & tomato 83
    mini burgers 147
    mushrooms, & thyme 89
    noodle stir-fry 150–1
    red pepper & carrot 83
    & sweet pepper 147
    tasty tagine 86–7
blueberry 102–3, 164–5
    apple & peach 41
    apple & pear crumble 166–7
    & banana 20
    nectarine & apple 162
    pear & banana 90–1
Bolognese, beef 88–9
bread 97
breakfasts 98, 100–4
broccoli 50, 60, 64, 135
burgers
    mini beef 147
    mini turkey 128–9
butternut squash 106–7
    baked 32–3
    carrot & apricot 42
    carrot & broccoli 64
    carrot & sweetcorn 49
    chicken & apricot 80–1
    parsnip, apple & prune 44
    pea & salmon risotto 139
    & plaice 74–5
    spinach & chicken 78
    spinach & peas 44
    & sweet potato 33
    sweet potato & pear 42
    tomato & chicken rice 117
    tomato & pepper 58–9

carrot 30–1, 33, 106–7
    & apple 46
    apple & spinach 63
    apricot & squash 42
    beef & red pepper 83
    broccoli & squash 64

chicken, pear & parsnip 79
cod, sweet potato & celery 76
orange & salmon 68–9
parsnip & apple 46
parsnip & celeriac 65
peas & beef 84
potato & sweetcorn 49
salmon & courgette 77
sweet potato & broccoli 50
sweetcorn & squash 49
tomato & cheese pasta 113
& tomato creamy pasta 114–15
casserole
    beef 82, 84
    chicken 120
cauliflower 64
celeriac 65
celery 76
cereals/grains 8, 55, 98
cheese 55, 98
    carrot & tomato pasta 113
    cheesy sauce 135
    chicken & tomato sandwich 156–7
    ham & tomato omelette 104
    lentil & tomato 66–7
    & scrambled egg 100–1
    tomato & chicken on toast 130–1
chewing 53
chicken 54
    apricot & squash 80–1
    casserole 120
    cheese & tomato on toast 130–1
    first curry 121
    Italian, & pasta 125
    & lentil curry 122–3
    mini sausages 126–7
    pear, parsnip & carrot 79
    squash & spinach 78

squash & tomato rice 117
& sweet potato mash 132
sweetcorn & tarragon pasta 133
tomato & cheese sandwich 156–7
tomato & spinach pasta 134
tomato & sweet pepper 79
choking 98
cod 76, 144–5
compote, fruit 102–3, 162
cooked purées 8
cottage pies, mini 148–9
courgette 60, 64, 77, 105–7
cream cheese 154–7, 159
crumble 166–7
curry, chicken 121–3

dairy products 10, 11, 55
dried fruit 97
drinks 10, 56

egg 10, 11, 98
    mayo, & tomato pinwheel 159
    omelette 104
    scrambled 100–1
equipment 13–14

finger foods 53, 55, 97, 154–71
first foods 8
fish 54, 68–77, 96, 135–45
fish cakes 138
food allergy 5, 10–12, 55–6
foods to avoid 10–11
freezing & reheating 12–13
fruit 54
    first purées 8, 16–21
fussy eaters 93

goujons, lemon sole 136–7

ham 104, 159

ice pops, berry yogurt 164-5
iron, dietary 7, 54, 96-7

kebabs, salmon 140-1

leek 65, 105
lemon sole 70-1, 136-7
lentil 62, 66-7, 83, 122-3

mango 26, 38-9
meal planners 15, 35, 57, 99
meat 54, 96
meatballs 146, 152-3
messy eaters 95-6
milk 7, 9-10, 96
muffins, mini 168-9
mushroom 89, 106-7
    pasta shells 111

nectarine 92, 162
noodle stir-fry, beef 150-1
nuts 10, 11, 55

omelettes 104
orange, salmon & carrot 68-9

papaya 8, 9, 22-3
parsnip 33, 82
    & apple 45
    apple, prune & squash 44
    apple & carrot 46
    broccoli & swede 60
    carrot, chicken & pear 79
    celeriac & carrot 65
    pear & swede 45
pasta 55, 97-8
    baby, salad 112
    beef Bolognese 88-9
    carrot, tomato, cheese 113
    chicken & sweetcorn 133
    chicken, tomato, spinach 134
    creamy carrot & tomato 114-15
    & Italian chicken 125
    mushroom shells 111
    tomato & veg sauce 110
pea
    beef & carrot 84
    leek & sweet potato 65
    salmon & squash risotto 139
    squash & spinach 44
    sweet potato & broccoli 50
peach 24-7, 38, 41
pear
    & apple 20
    apple & blueberry crumble 166-7
    apple & plum porridge 163
    & apricot 93
    apricot & apple porridge 92
    banana & blueberry 90-1
    parsnip, carrot & chicken 79
    purée, cream of 16-17
    raisin & apple 36
    squash & sweet potato 42
    swede & parsnip 45
pepper 58-60, 79, 83, 147
pies, cod & sweetcorn 144-5
pinwheels 159
pizza tortilla wedges 160-1
plaice with squash 74-5
plum, pear & apple porridge 163
porridge 92-3, 102-3, 163
potato 49, 148-9
premature infants 5
prune 44
pulses 55

raisin, apple & pear 36
raspberry 102-3, 164-5
raw purées 8-9, 22-9
rice 108-9, 117, 139
risotto, salmon 139
rusks 97, 170-1

salad, baby pasta 112
salmon
    broccoli & cheese sauce 135
    carrot & orange 68-9
    courgette & carrot 77
    & dill 73
    marinated kebabs 140-1
    nuggets 142-3
    squash & pea risotto 139
    sweet potato, tomato & basil 72
salt 10-11
sandwiches 154-7
sausages, mini chicken 126-7
self-feeding 53, 55, 95-8, 154-71
spinach
    carrot & apple 63
    chicken & squash 78
    chicken & tomato pasta 134
    courgette & cauliflower 64
    & lemon sole 70-1
    pea & squash 44
    swede & apple 41
stir-fry, beef noodle 150-1
strawberry 26-7, 36-7, 164-5
swede 41, 45, 60
sweet & sour sauce 136-7
sweet potato 33, 86-7
    & apple muffins 168-9
    aubergine & tomato 116
    baked 32
    broccoli & carrot 50
    broccoli & peas 50
    celery, carrot & cod 76
    courgette & leek 105
    mash 132
    pea & leek 65
    pear & squash 42
    & squash, baked 33
    tomato, basil & salmon 72
    wedges 118-19
sweetcorn
    carrot & potato 49
    & chicken pasta 133
    & cod pies 144-5
    squash & carrot 49
    & tuna fish cakes 138

tagine, tasty beef 86-7
teething 98
toast 130-1
tomato 60, 160-1
    beef & lentils 83
    & carrot creamy pasta 114-15
    cheese & carrot pasta 113
    cheese & chicken sandwich 156-7
    cheese & ham omelette 104
    cheese & lentil 66-7
    chicken & cheese on toast 130-1
    chicken & squash rice 117
    & egg mayo pinwheels 159
    pepper & chicken 79
    pepper & squash 58-9
    salmon & sweet potato 72
    scrambled egg 100-1
    spinach & chicken pasta 134
    sweet potato & aubergine 116
    & veg pasta sauce 152-3
    & veg sauce 110
tortilla pizza wedges 160-1
tuna sweetcorn fish cakes 138
turkey, mini burgers 128-9

vegetables 54, 97
    first purées 8, 30-3
    Mediterranean 60-1
    mini balls 106-7
    & tomato sauce 110
vegetarian diet 56

water 10
when to wean 5-6

yogurt berry ice pops 164-5

Growing up with Annabel Karmel
Books for every stage of your child's development.

As a parent, giving your child a healthy start in life is a top priority. Annabel offers a cookbook for every stage of your child's development. As the UK's number one bestselling author on cooking for babies and children, Annabel's tried and tested recipes and meal planners have proved invaluable to families for over 20 years.

Pregnancy
- Eating for Two

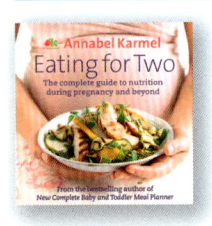

Family
- Annabel Karmel's Complete Family Meal Planner
- 100 Family Meals
- Annabel's Family Cookbook

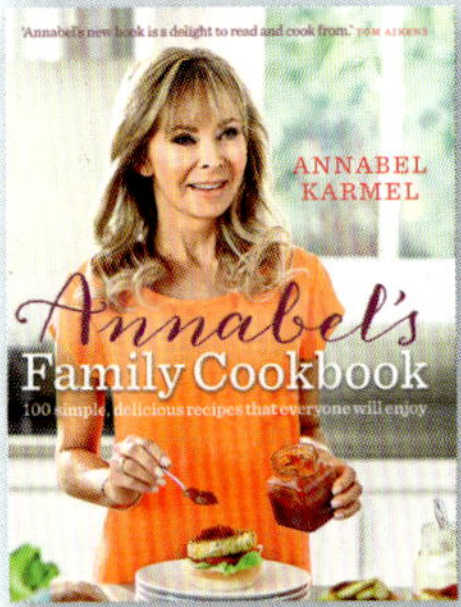

Baby and Toddler
- Annabel Karmel's New Complete Baby and Toddler Meal Planner
- Complete First Year Planner
- Top 100 Meals in Minutes
- Top 100 Pasta Dishes
- Top 100 Finger Foods
- Top 100 Baby Purées
- Superfoods for Babies and Children
- Quick & Easy Toddler Recipes

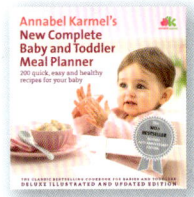

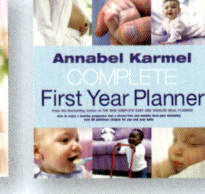

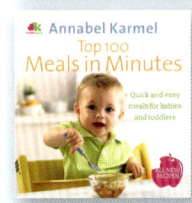

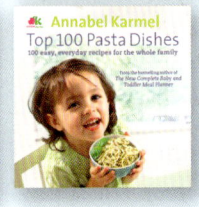

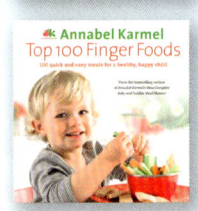

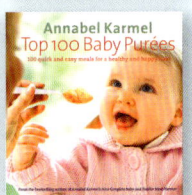

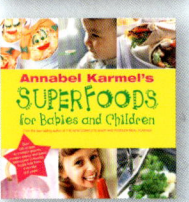

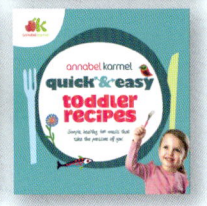

School age/cooking for kids
- Princess Party Cookbook
- Lunchboxes
- The Fussy Eaters' Recipe Book
- Annabel's Kitchen: My First Cookbook
- Complete Party Planner

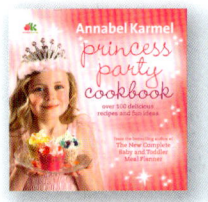

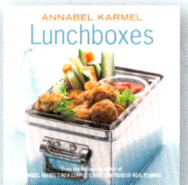

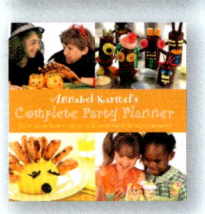

For more information go to **www.annabelkarmel.com**

annabel karmel

About the author

Annabel Karmel is the UK's bestselling author on baby and children's food and nutrition. She is the number one parenting author and an expert in creating delicious healthy meals for children without spending hours in the kitchen.

Her previous books have sold more than 4 million copies worldwide and *The Complete Baby and Toddler Meal Planner* regularly features in the top 5 cookery titles.

Annabel was awarded an MBE in June 2006 in the Queen's Birthday Honours for her outstanding work in the field of child nutrition.

Acknowledgements

I would like to thank the following for their help and work on this book: Dave King for his beautiful photography. Emma Lahaye for food styling and props. Lucinda McCord for recipe testing. Smith & Gilmour for design. Gwénola Carrère for illustrations.

Sarah Smith for all her enthusiasm and support. The team at Ebury Press including Fiona MacIntyre, Lizzy Gray, Helena Caldon, Ursula Elliott, Lucy Harrison and Sarah Bennie.

My wonderful models Aiyana, Megan, Fennella, Matilda, Mylo, Poppy and Lola.

Lastly but not least I would like to thank my children Nicholas, Lara and Scarlett.

The essentials you need for bringing up a happy, healthy baby

Annabel's Essential Guide to Feeding Your Baby & Toddler now offers instant access to more than 200 delicious recipes, as well as a host of features including weekly planners, shopping lists, a kitchen timer, recipe notes, videos and lots more.

Download from the App Store now

Have you tried Annabel's range of Organic Baby Purees and Organic Sauces? These scrumptious flavour combinations contain nothing but pure, wholesome goodness and taste just like home-made – perfect for tiny tums.
Look out for our Organic Sauces too!
Available in supermarkets nationwide

www.annabelkarmel.com